11-WEEK LANGUAGE FACILITATION JOURNEY TO SPEECH

A WORKBOOK FOR PARENTS AND CAREGIVERS OF LATE TALKERS

Guided, Step-by-Step Process to Facilitate Unprompted Spoken Language

Including Data Collection Journal to Document Progress

Second Edition - 2022 Update

by Marci Melzer, Intuitive SLP
Language Facilitation Consultant
WAVESOFCOMMUNICATION.COM

WavesofCommunication.com

To request permissions contact the author
Marci@WavesofCommunication.com

ISBN 979-8-88526-445-7

Thank you!

This workbook is inspired by thousands of parents and caregivers of late talkers around the world. The process you will learn in this workbook has evolved through my work with real families who were failing to help shift functional communication from behaviors, crying, and scripted words into REAL speech.

The parents who have bravely trusted themselves as language facilitators and **focused on their process instead of progress** finally found the speech they were looking for.

The results of your own work provides the evidence that parents and caregivers have the potential to facilitate <u>unlimited</u> spoken language success.

Marci Melzer
Waves of Communication Founder

POSSIBILITIES USING THIS BOOK

Greater Connection Through Mutual Understanding

It is my intention for this tool to guide your everyday practice as you naturally, intuitively connect with the late talker in the 'Language Facilitation Zone' and systematically help them shift their nonverbal communication into ever-evolving functional spoken language.

Create Functional Goals to Increase Abilities

You will create realistic goals based on the current abilities of the late talker and use them as a guide to establish a daily routine that is naturally full of opportunities for you to practice language facilitation.

Keep Motivated for Consistent Progress

Quick self-check analysis tools will help you realize how your thoughts and actions directly affect the late talker's efforts toward switching from behaviors into speech. Learn what works and give up what doesn't.

Evolve Your Skills Together to Avoid Plateau

Weekly review will help you evolve your language models and remain confident as you encourage the late talker to make new effort every day toward speech improvement.

Have FUN and Feel Happy EVERY Day

Journaling with this workbook will help you maintain a positive mindset AND forward progress in speech as you navigate all of the natural energetic highs and lows you will experience on your language facilitation journey.

Document and Share Your Results

Your entries in this workbook/journal will accumulate data to share with others regarding the late talker's progress toward functional spoken language success as well as the strategies and dedicated action that worked to facilitate the best outcomes.

Table of Contents

Introduction

Section One - Analysis

Section 2 - Planning

Section 3- Take Action

Section 4- Level Up

Section 5- Your Journal

Understanding Language Facilitation

What does the term 'Late-Talker' mean?
Late-Talker is the term I use for ANYONE who does not feel proficient at using spoken language to communicate their needs and ideas effectively wherever they live, work, and play every day. All humans who can hear speech level sounds, have unrestricted mouth movement, and consciously connect with other people have the capacity to develop understanding and functional use at least some level of spoken language.

What is the role / responsibility of the language facilitator?
Language facilitators can take a big lesson from **social media influencers**. Late talkers learn like we ALL do. They quickly become eager to **follow** and even <u>imitate</u> the people who they look up to and admire. Language facilitators take on the role as **influencer** to help the late talker make a shift in the way that they communicate habitually. To be successful, just like a social media influencer, the effective language facilitator takes the time and effort to KNOW their follower well before they release content. They also pay attention to trends and shift their message accordingly.

Language facilitators also serve the role of **interpreter and translator**. They are trained by the late talker to understand their communication behaviors to 'know' and respond to their wants, needs, struggles etc. and share those messages with other people who don't understand them.

How do language facilitators know what to say?
Your connection with the late talker allows you to understand their messages and integrate their ideas into your own spoken language **productions**. Just like social content creators, Language Facilitators take the responsibility to make their **content** (speech models) seem so EASY, HAPPY, SAFE, and FUN, that their followers can't get enough of watching and participating.

What's required for language facilitators to see progress?
Language facilitators must have patience and trust in the process. Like social media influencers, your job is to connect, produce content, and TRUST that your language models will inspire speech **without expectation of immediate performance.** If your message resonates, the late talker will **follow** along, show that they **like** what you're doing, and hopefully, **comment with speech** they are inspired.

What to Expect When You Use Language Facilitation Strategies

A Mindset Shift - The Source of Language is YOU

The worldwide followers on my Waves of Communication platform have reported the first thing they experienced when starting language facilitation is a big change in their mindset. The connection you create will help you develop a whole new understanding of the late talker's experience. You will realize how powerful your actions are and that there is nobody better than you and loving family/friends to teach the late talker how to talk. You will understand that your language facilitation opportunities are their BEST chance at learning natural, conversational spoken language.

Better Listening, Attention, and Participation

When you commit to creating (at least) one, conscious language facilitation experience every day you can expect your efforts to be rewarded with better attention and listening, starting within the first few days. This workbook shows you how to create opportunities all day long for more intensive intervention.

Spontaneous Imitation of Actions and Speech

Late talkers will try to imitate your actions and speech when they TRUST you to help them succeed through demonstration and coaching (and without prompting, forcing, or hand-over-hand guidance). The truth is, most late talkers want to learn HOW language works and they have been waiting for you to teach them the words THEY need. Late talkers can't resist fun opportunities to explore the things they like and are happy to put in extra effort to overcome challenges and try new skills that they believe will equip and empower them for success.

Happiness Through SELF Empowerment

This workbook intends to help evolve your natural abilities. You will develop habits to instantly connect, translate nonverbal messages and then intuitively know exactly what to do and say. You will respond with confidence and grace even when you feel emotionally exhausted or triggered by outside influences.

You will become a natural language facilitator!

Characteristics of an Effective Language Facilitator

MINDSET MATTERS

Accept that YOU are part of creating your current communication situation.
Regardless of the root cause of the late-talking, every new event affects learning and development of communication. How have YOU contributed to the current level?

Take responsibility to be the catalyst of change.
Language facilitators must be flexible in the ways that you connect and model speech. This is how you will learn to ride through all of the energetic ups and downs that are typical in late talker's life. Your everyday activities will become much more successful as you take the time to connect to their current energy before you start coaching through the skills.

Give up strategies and interventions that BLOCK your child's speech.
The only way to get a different (better) outcome is to take NEW action that you feel inspired and happy to do every day. You will know if your strategies are working by the happy connection you feel with the late talker. Testing and prompting beyond your natural language models feels very low-energy and desperate. It also sends the subconscious (low-vibe) message that you do not trust in the language facilitation process and will trigger failures.

Make gratitude your daily goal.
You are blessed with the opportunity to connect and nurture the beautiful soul that lies within the late talker who you love. Every night before sleep, appreciate how you were able to affect the late talker's efforts that day. Remind yourself of how, because of your facilitation, they tried a little harder and achieved some small success. Always appreciate the effort that has been made and you will stay away from mindset traps of focus on failure or worry.

Facilitate language 2-3 hours (total) EVERY day
Language facilitator parents learn to "work" with their child's speech everywhere. Every large event and small happy or sad moment is another opportunity to facilitate spoken language. In the moment, you can model functional language to talk about feelings and negotiate the environment more easily than in structured sessions. Talk about ALL experiences you share together with your whole family. If you don't know what to do, it's time to connect with the late talker and they will guide you to an activity that they want you to talk about.

Have FUN and ENJOY language learning together
If it isn't FUN it ISN'T fun. That's true about everything when it comes to connection and learning. Fun is important for both the facilitator and the late talker. No more HARD WORK at MAKING your child do and say things that they don't want to! It's time to teach your child how to have FUN overcoming challenges and learning new things so they FEEL successful.

7 LEVELS OF LANGUAGE FACILITATOR MINDSET

Language Facilitation Zone

LEVEL 7

Inspired to Involve Others

Inviting everyone you encounter into the language facilitation zone where active listening provides inspiration to encourage discussion.

LEVEL 6

Patient and Trusting in the Process

Taking time to plan and facilitate ideas over time. Focus on your own effort instead of judgement of results. Past success is the fuel to keep working.

LEVEL 5

Describing Everything You Think

Intuitively connected and aware that the late talker is listening and processing. Saying every thought out loud to model speech you want to hear.

Equal Give and Take

Focusing on shifting needs-based behaviors into labels for the objects and actions that the late talker needs to make life easier on everybody.

 *Progress Begins Here* 

LEVEL 3

Stuck in Old Habits

Worrying about lack of progress creates panic and focus on what is NOT developing. Prompting and bribing speech output to experience success.

LEVEL 2

Overwhelmed/Frustrated

Shutting down conscious action due to over-reliance on outside influences. Lack of trust that you have the ability to overcome your problems.

LEVEL 1

Discouraged /Doubtful

Feeling completely defeated. Overcome with grief over loss of healthy child and happy life. Fear that you will have a future full of sadness.

SECTION

01

ANALYZING SPOKEN LANGUAGE DEVELOPMENT

Language development is a complex process. This section details 7 levels of natural evolution across 3 focus areas. Progress in EACH of the focus areas is necessary for late talkers to make the shift from nonverbal communication to developing their best unprompted spoken language.

- **Connection and trust** in the *language facilitation zone*
- **Understanding / processing** of spoken language
- Functional expression **using speech as the primary mode**

These levels can serve as your reference guide as you collect data for self analysis and progress reporting.

Why is Analysis So Important?

Understand overall functional spoken language ability without testing
Late talkers make up their own 'language' of communication behaviors to use with parents and caregivers. As you connect with the late talker's energy during everyday interactions, you will observe their typical communication behaviors and develop a clear understanding of their habitual communication methods. Your daily snapshot analysis will reveal, step-by-step, the late talker's journey of progress through the levels of spoken language development.

Discover the late talkers abilities and wisdom
Analysis also helps facilitators discover functional talents, knowledge, and skills (such as using technology) that standardized testing doesn't give credit for. Smart language facilitators will use the late talker's hidden skills and knowledge to evolve their FUN language facilitation opportunities beyond basic imitation and programming to skyrocket their functional results.

Learn how to achieve better outcomes
Intuitive observation and analysis helps facilitators identify the strategies that work well and those that the late talker does not appreciate. Over time, you will observe the late talker's favorite, and most effective learning activities. You will also learn what tips, and tricks to have ready just in case the late talker is triggered by outside influences. Analysis helps you to stay one step ahead of the late talker and provide the support they need for consistently great experiences. Consistent feelings of success help your whole family feel happy every day and continue to work hard to facilitate the spoken language everybody wants to hear!

Facilitate neural plasticity through holistic analysis and intervention
Neurological development of each sub-area in the spoken language system is equally important for necessary for natural, unprompted, self-directed spoken language to emerge. Connection with the facilitator, and motivation to self-improve are areas often overlooked in the intervention plan, in favor of prompting and rewarding speech output. The most effective language facilitators maintain a high level of intuitive communication connection, and empower self-motivation to evolve behaviors into speech. That process creates new neurological pathways for functional spoken language success.

Elevate your loving connection as well as spoken language results
The individual areas of connection/motivation to talk, listening, and speaking, rarely develop at the same rate. Late talkers often move up or down in each individual level quickly as a direct result of their experiences with the people they love. Analysis provides the evidence. So, you can realize how your dedicated language facilitation interventions consciously affect changes in the late talker's social communication and loving connection with you and others.

Resources for Analysis

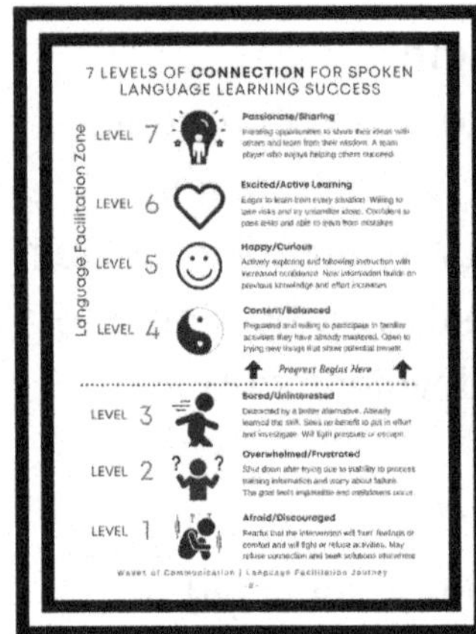

Level Reference Charts

These charts provide a snapshot of typical functional spoken language development progression that you can achieve with natural language facilitation. A graphic helps language facilitators visually understand each level of development from the perspective of the late talker.

Use the charts for quick reference as you record your daily experiences. Share them as a visual tool to explain the late talker's spoken language abilities to others.

Detailed Explanation of the levels

The levels are fully explained so language facilitators can become familiar with what to expect as you work together. Examples of typical communication behaviors at each level will inspire your starting point and help you create goals. Daily analysis helps you continually focus toward taking the right action to achieve the highest potential of spoken language. You will develop new habits that keep your mindset positive and avoid traps that block your progress.

Your Home Videos - Profile / Analysis Forms

It is easier to complete objective analysis when you are able to observe typical communication situations from an outside point of view. Language facilitators are advised to use video to record your interactions often. With ongoing weekly review of and analysis of your videos, you can record the late talker's progression. Your data provides the evidence of your results.

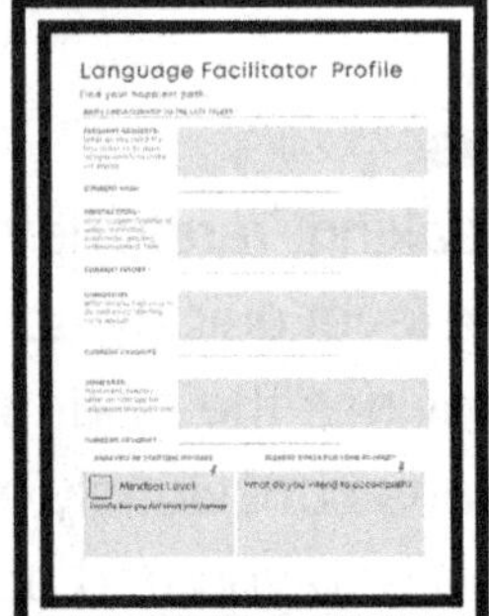

You will also learn which language facilitation opportunities feel good AND work well to get your desired outcomes. Your evidence will help you quit giving away your energy to those ineffective strategies that you can prove are no longer helpful to facilitate unprompted, independent, functional speech.

Find the Language Facilitation Zone

The Energetic 'Space' Where Intuitive Connection Naturally Facilitates Speech Development

---

Translate EVERYTHING you 'know' into language models
Parents and caregivers, are naturally very familiar with the late talker's habits, preferences, and emotional triggers. This is why you can easily interpret even the most subtle and intuitive communication and facilitate evolution of the behaviors into speech. '*You really enjoy watching music videos. You want to watch them ALL day.*'

Share the feelings you perceive. As you focus on your CONNECTION, you will learn to understand experiences from the late talker's unique perspective. In the language facilitation zone, you FEEL 'tuned in' to the energy behind nonverbal communication behaviors so you can intelligently understand specific ideas, even when they are being communicated through aggression or cuddles, screaming or flapping hands. '*You are really upset. You want more tablet time and I took it away.*'

Use your connection to regulate emotions. You will naturally 'know' EXACTLY how to find calm when chaos is triggered by outside influences if you simply take a minute and find your connection with the late talker in the language facilitation zone. Over time using this 'space' will become your habit to facilitate better communication with everyone you meet. '*It's a bummer that video time is over. I know you feel sad now. let's hug it out. Tomorrow we will have more video time after lunch. Help me put the tablet on the charger. Now, let's go for a walk outside and we can sing!*'

Expand attention, focus, and trust. Depending on the late talker's anxiety level, you may only facilitate a few seconds of attention at first. You will need to provide EASY and/or FUN opportunities for **A total of 2-3 hours EVERY day** before a late talker will decide to TRUST you to NURTURE their feelings, wishes, and ideas as THEY try to talk. **Your patience and trust in the process** will encourage the transformation from behavior into real speech and language. '*Watch me, it's FUN! Baby Shark do do do...*'

7 LEVELS OF **CONNECTION** WITH THE LANGUAGE FACILITATOR

Language Facilitation Zone

LEVEL 7

Passionate/ Grateful Sharing

Initiating opportunities to share their ideas with others and learn from their wisdom. A team player who enjoys helping others succeed.

LEVEL 6

Excited/Active Exchange

Eager to learn from every situation. Willing to take risks and try unfamiliar ideas. Confident to pass tests and able to learn from mistakes.

LEVEL 5

Happy/Curious Exploring

Actively exploring and following instruction with increased confidence. New information builds on previous knowledge and effort increases.

LEVEL 4

Content/Balanced Tolerance

Regulated and willing to participate in familiar activities they have already mastered. Open to trying new things that show potential benefit.

 *Progress Begins Here* 

LEVEL 3

Bored/Uninterested Escape

Distracted by a better alternative. Already learned the skill. Topic or activity is unappealing. Fighting pressure and/or manipulating to get their way.

LEVEL 2

Overwhelmed/Frustrated Quitting

Shut down. Unable to connect with others due to low self confidence. Focused on mental ideas of suffering loss/failure. All effort seems a waste.

LEVEL 1

Afraid/Discouraged Sadness

Fearful that the facilitator will 'hurt' feelings or comfort. Fight or flee activities. May refuse all connection and isolate physically or in their mind.

7 LEVELS OF FUNCTIONAL SPOKEN LANGUAGE **UNDERSTANDING**

LEVEL 7

Understanding Others' Perspective

Understands how spoken language affects feelings. Active listening to show empathy for others and learn how to help them.

LEVEL 6

Focus for structured learning

Attentive for group listening and able to remember and practice the information shared. Listening for specific information to pass tests.

LEVEL 5

Independently Expanding Knowledge

If/then understanding happens through repeated testing and experimentation. Big increase in vocabulary identification and following directions.

LEVEL 4

Following Directions and Rules

Learning the rules through understanding of their benefit. Listens carefully to memorize words that they can use to share specific needs and ideas.

Spoken Language Processing Begins Here

LEVEL 3

Testing/Discernment

Attentive to people and situations they can trust to give more info than test. Seeking independent opportunity to explore. - Will avoid pressure.

LEVEL 2

Joint Attention/First Listening

Aware that others can help them understand things they are confused about, meet their needs, and work through their emotions.

LEVEL 1

Awareness/Discrimination

Listening for volume and tone to gain information behind speech sounds. Using visual information to understand labels for people and objects.

7 LEVELS OF FUNCTIONAL SPOKEN LANGUAGE **EXPRESSION**

LEVEL 7

Confident Expression of Unique Ideas

Using speech as a primary mode to connect with others and converse in detail about topics. Asking questions to access knowledge and instruct others.

LEVEL 6

Expression of Abilities / Negotiation

Ability to access knowledge and answer questions verbally. Solve problems using speech instead of behavior. Speech clarity improves.

LEVEL 5

Social Language / Sharing Ideas

Using speech to share personal opinions and express feelings regarding success and disappointment. Talking about experiences.

LEVEL 4

Functional Needs-Based Speech

Talking to express needs including specifics and still using behaviors for big emotions or complex ideas they haven't learned vocabulary for yet.

 *Functional Spoken Language Begins Here* 

LEVEL 3

Parroting / Limited-Function Speech

Imitation of favorite or useful words and phrases that relate to interests. Label objects to request. Will say meaningless words to get rewards.

LEVEL 2

Specific Nonverbal Behaviors

Pantomime, pointing, and dragging caregivers to communicate wants and needs. First pop out words to label favorite objects and people.

LEVEL 1

Emotional/Subconscious Expression

Nonverbal sounds crying, whining, cooing, and laughing to express general feelings and overall energy and help caregivers guess wants/needs.

Find Your Current Level

7 LEVELS OF **CONNECTION** FOR SPOKEN LANGUAGE SUCCESS

Level 01

Afraid / Discouraged - Fight or Flight

At this stage, the late talker is completely isolated in self-preservation mode. They do not trust that anyone (including themselves) can help solve their problems and wish for some miracle to come and rescue them from suffering.

No new learning can happen because concentration is on the suffering and not the solution. Facilitators will observe chaotic communication, with complete meltdowns, falling to the floor, screaming, and other seemingly random communication that appears reflexive, such as ear holding, hand flapping, toe walking, mouthing objects, and hitting are used to communicate deep physical or emotional feelings that others can't see. These are all subconscious communication messages for the language facilitator to interpret into speech models.

Level 02

Overwhelmed / Frustrated - Feeling Ignored or Abandoned

The late talker slides into this level when they have been trying their best to communicate a message and they have failed. This level is triggered when caregivers either ignore nonverbal communication messages, or they say 'no, don't, or stop' in response. The late talker is using behavior to request something that was previously allowed and they do not understand why they cannot have their wish. When the late talker's expectations are not immediately met (seemingly without reason), they slip into a mindset of loss and frustration, or limitation to their freedom. *'That's not fair!'*

At this stage, the late talker may use repeated behaviors to try to convince the facilitator to change their mind. Communication tries at this stage are poorly executed, because the late talker is upset and frustrated. Those late talkers who have said words will often resort back to tantrums and nonverbal gestures to communicate their feelings because they are not able to calmly access the language they have learned.

When late talkers experience disagreement to their messages, they do not feel 'heard' or understood and will 'shut down' the connection with those who disagree and find others who will respond in the way they want. Connection can be regained in the language facilitation zone with understanding, compromise, and negotiation for a win-win outcome.

Levels of Connection

Level 03

Bored / Uninterested - Looking for Something Better

This level is triggered when the late talker feels the experience offered to them is less beneficial than any alternate experience they could find or create on their own. Late talkers live in the NOW. They judge every opportunity in the moment as it occurs to FEEL if the experience 'resonates' with their current energy. If the late talker sees or hears input that is fun and excites their curiosity, they will connect and respond. However, if the late talker hears or sees something they have already experienced, they will compare it against their current experience and always choose the opportunity that helps them feel better.

ACTIONS MATTER Late talkers who feel pressure to perform repeated activities will eventually resist these activities and try to escape from them. Often, the late talker will turn the avoidance and escape into a game that is actually helpful to elevate the connection by turning the tables and encouraging the facilitator to watch and respond to their behaviors. Smart language facilitators will pick up on this cue and try a new alternative to teaching their concept that is more entertaining and functional from the perspective of the late talker.

Level 04

Content / Balanced - Receptive to Connection

This level is where the language facilitation zone begins. There is an established trust that the facilitator will consistently offer an open opportunity to connect intuitively and understand the late talker's deepest ideas, without judgement, even when their spoken language fails them and they use behaviors that they do not like.

Language facilitators can enjoy more eye contact as well as joint attention for the new information they are sharing via language models. Listening happens even when the late talker is not looking. You may notice that the late talker is always wanting to be nearby and 'listening in' when you are talking to other people. They may notice and touch your mouth.

Late talkers will use behaviors and first speech attempts as their way to prompt you to talk more at this stage. The late talker's brain is like a sponge, and you are helping them fill their memory banks with information and language models they can use later to communicate their own messages. They will want to connect as often as possible when you are talking.

Levels of Connection

Level 05

Happy to Listen / Curious to Try

The late talker is now able appreciate the connection with their caregivers as a result of the many, consistently helpful teaching and language opportunities they have experienced together. They trust that you are the source of their knowledge and establish your role as their guide. These late talkers are consistently seeking a stronger connection with facilitators and coaches to actively expand their knowledge about the topics they are interested in.

Your connection has proven to the late talker that you will understand and support their efforts as they reach beyond their comfort zone and try to imitate your language models. They pay close attention and follow instructions with commitment to improve their functional communication success and make their teachers proud.

Level 06

Excited to Connect / Rapid Learning Happens

At this level, the late talker is seeking connections wherever they go. They understand that anyone, who will make the effort to connect, is a potential source of knowledge or opportunity. Late talkers understand the give-and-take of communication and are more open to following rules.

Social friendships are building and late talkers may pick up behaviors, gestures, noises, words, or phrases that they hear from their peers and influencers. Late talkers are able to see the benefit that other people get from paying attention and trying hard to be the best they can be.

IMPORTANT This is the level where competition or obsession can replace a true learning connection. Late talkers can develop an obsessive attraction to repeat their favorite experiences and exclude new ideas. Language facilitators should keep focus on functional learning experiences and personal achievements to demonstrate that there progress happening a little more every day. Smart language facilitators will TRUST that the late talker is learning and focus on celebrating every EFFORT toward everyday self improvement instead of testing results and pushing the late talker to work hard on reaching the next level of progress.

Levels of Connection

Level 07

Passionate Connection / Empathy for Others

At this level the late talker understands that their actions have affect on others. They will initiate opportunities to share their ideas and request feedback. Open to shifting their mindset and behavior when they understand the wants and needs of the people they care about. This late talker is a team player who enjoys helping others succeed and will even push through communication barriers to help their loved ones solve problems.

Parents and caregivers may notice the late talker's empathy as they respond with kind actions when others are sad. They will try very hard to do whatever they can to make you feel happy. Motivation to work hard may be noticed by parents and caregivers who consistently show appreciation for the specific ways the late talker's development helps the family.

- 'Wow, you are such a good helper. Thank you for bringing me your dishes.'
- *'I love how you are listening and working so hard.'*
- *'It makes me happy that we understand each other and don't fight about things anymore.'*

Find Your Current Level

7 LEVELS OF **UNDERSTANDING** AND PROCESSING SPOKEN LANGUAGE

Level 01

Awareness of other people talking to them

At this stage the late talker is able to process facial expressions and body language as well as energetic vibration (mood) and messages behind changes in pitch, volume, and rhythm of speech in familiar speakers. The brain is just developing to understand how communication works. The late talker is able to understand that people have an identity and relationship to them, however, they are very self-serving focused at this stage and do not have any real attention, outside of fleeting surprise, shock or delight.

At this stage, the late talker is able to follow nonverbal cues to understand basic spoken language messages about their personal needs and immediate environment. They have identified what objects, people, and activities help them meet their needs and rely on their physical body reactions to know if something is good or bad. The late talker is learning how to watch behavior of others and learn from them. Young kids are learning to walk during this stage. Late talkers of all ages are typically hyper-focused on problem solving and navigation of their environment to try to independently access the experiences they want. Therefore, they are poor listeners.

Level 02

Joint attention toward a common topic with the facilitator

This is the stage where the late talker becomes inspired to start listening. They have learned that the facilitator is the source of interesting knowledge and trust that they consistently offer fun opportunities to learn new things without pressure to perform. Late talkers at this stage are eager to investigate, participate, and even overcome small challenges when the facilitator's language facilitation opportunities feel inviting and the facilitator feels supported.

While eager to explore, the late talker is still ego-driven and will only pay attention and listen carefully to information that they believe will help them succeed to solve a problem or make them feel happy and safe. Attention span may vary widely depending on the late talker's level of understanding and confidence with the task at hand. They may be able to watch videos or play with parents for hours, however, they may resist playing together with unfamiliar toys or people, especially when they feel pressure to perform.

Levels of Understanding and Processing

Level 03

Exploring and testing limits of knowledge

The late talker is now able to interpret the intent behind others' nonverbal communication and identify patterns of caregivers' behavior to learn how to manipulate them. They learn how their own communication behaviors cause caregivers to respond both positively and negatively. Fearless exploring, and limits testing are common. This stage marks the beginning of the late talker's understanding of how it feels to be self empowered as well as the experience of loss of control. Late talkers who are strong-willed learn to quickly change their behavior to fight back for control by pushing caregiver's buttons through changes in eating, sleeping, escaping, or making messes that trigger an emotional response.

This is the stage where the late talker is learning communication 'works' by watching how others do it. They listen and watch for both nonverbal and verbal messages that work for others to manipulate their environment and get the things they want. Late talkers are now highly motivated by 'rewards' for showing their skills, and therefore will learn new vocabulary quickly at this stage. Late talkers can point out pictured objects and actions, as well as colors, shapes, animals etc. They start to follow step-by-step directions, especially with a physical cue and can also learn to respond to prompting questions that most facilitators are asking as they teach, test, and reward the memorization of new vocabulary and following directions.

Level 04

Following rules and participating in regular routines

At this stage the late talker can apply previously learned knowledge to familiar routines and common situations they encounter. They have learned that when they listen and understand what is expected of them, they can take the right action to follow the rules. Better effort toward listening typically naturally causes language facilitators to reduce their own reactive nonverbal behavior and take the time to explain things and providing appropriate models.

Life gets happier at home because the late talker listens better and has moved past the self-serving mindset into being a team player and follow rules for the good of the household. They realize that when life isn't easy and FUN, the alternative is sad and frustrating. There is less power struggle and fighting at this stage and more understanding of how the late talker contributes to the environment. Tantrums and running away turns into helpful participation.

Levels of Understanding and Processing

Level 05

Trial and error learning to expand current language

The late talker is now able to consider previous experiences and make changes to set new goals for future development. They know what's going on now so confidence builds. Late talkers are finding self reliance at this stage and learning who they can trust. If/then understanding happens through repeated testing and experimentation with new levels of exploration. Negotiation to compromise the rules becomes an option as the late talker realizes that there are endless possibilities as long as they can keep exploring and testing.

IMPORTANT NOTE This is the stage when late talkers learn about written verbal language and start to figure out that letters have sounds and those letters and sounds can be combined in infinite ways using patterns to create a language. Some late talkers may become hyper focused on reading as a way to communicate at this stage if they grasp the idea behind printed words have meaning and they visually memorize more easily than listening. Spoken language models will help visually-inclined learners develop listening too.

Level 06

Following stories and understanding feelings behind experiences discussing memories

The late talker is hyper-focused on self improvement and also very self-conscious about their success, or lack of it. They may be super attentive to speakers and maybe looking at/touching their own or people's mouths when they talk. The late talker at this stage always enjoys when others talk slowly and repeat themselves. They light up when someone says something they want to try to say for themselves and often will imitate the word or phrase immediately. At this stage, the late talker is able to attend well, follow complex directions and remember multi-step processes to create an outcome.

IMPORTANT NOTE Late talkers can be very self-conscious about their own speech and communication behavior trials and errors at this stage and they become aware that others are judging them. Experiences where speech is consistently prompted or the late talker's efforts are always corrected cause them the feel inadequate in their effort to try. It is very easy for late talkers to hyper focus on what they have done wrong and feel defeated when judged by others. Without consistent encouragement and support from the language facilitator, the late talker may regress and stop talking.

Levels of Understanding and Processing Spoken Language

Level 7

Being able to see things from someone else's perspective

The new talker now understands that there are consequences to their actions and words. They are able to relate to the feelings of others when they talk about feeling happy or sad and understand what circumstances caused those feelings to happen.

At this stage, the new talker listens to investigate WHY and HOW everything is happening around them. Now that they are self-empowered with basic skills, the new talker is motivated to improve their own spoken language. This is the stage where storytelling and pretend play are the source of learning. Cognitive development is happening constantly with new mind-blowing discoveries every day.

At this stage, the child will prompt their facilitators to talk more and provide them with additional information to learn the reasons, opinions, and drama behind the experiences they are exploring. High level of integration and processing is happening as the late talker can remember experiences and benefit from coaching. They also can observe and learn lessons from other's mistakes just as as easily as they learn from their own.

Find Your Current Level

7 LEVELS OF FUNCTIONAL SPOKEN LANGUAGE **EXPRESSION**

Level 01

Emotion-based (subconscious) expression

This is the most basic level of expressive communication used by newborn babies. Typical communication behaviors at this stage include a range of crying, whining, cooing, and laughing to express general feelings and overall energy. The verbal behaviors are designed to help caregivers intuitively understand the late talker's wants and needs so that you can help them consistently feel calm and happy.

As they have new experiences, the late talker will elevate their communication, relying on caregivers to intuitively guess their more elevated wants and needs. This is the stage where late talkers use big communication behaviors for big feelings. It is common to see behaviors pop up out of nowhere, especially those intended to cause those around them to FEEL their feelings. Some examples are screeching, hitting, biting for sad feelings and flapping, jumping, and running around when they are happy. Subconscious facial expressions and physical reactions (poopy diaper, throwing up, screaming) are the nonverbal communication messages that the late talker at this stage relies on for caregivers to interpret and respond to.

Level 02

Experimentation with nonverbal and verbal methods

At this stage, the late talker is focusing on making sure others understand their exact demands. You may observe more advanced nonverbal communication behaviors such as grumpy facial expressions, pointing at specific objects, pantomime behaviors they want you to perform, and physical guidance as they push you around, move your hands and guide your body as their 'language' to prompt you to do and say what they want.

You may hear the late talker playing with vocal sounds for entertainment (humming/babbling). First tries at speech-like jargon and surprise ‘pop out’ words may appear when the late talker is playing and exploring but they will not be used consistently because the late talker is primarily focused on exploring and recognizing what they like and don't like.

Late talkers may be very active at this stage because they are spending a lot of energy trying (and failing) to communicate the ideas that they are thinking about with images and sounds they make with their physical body.

Levels of Functional Spoken Language Expression

Level 03

Spontaneous imitation - 'parroting'

The late talker's neurological spoken language system is starting to develop and now speech is available as a new expressive tool. The late talker is 'trying out' how it feels to talk at this stage and they are now keenly aware of how others are responding to their communication behaviors and speech attempts. You may commonly hear words the late talker finds attractive such as family or favorite character names, colors, numbers, shapes, animals, vehicles, etc. combined with a variety of experimental vocal sounds (jargon/babbling), word approximations, and phrases that the late talker has heard others use in videos, songs, and during their everyday experiences with language facilitators.

IMPORTANT Late talkers are very responsive to bribery at this stage and those who are offered a 'reinforcement' in exchange for saying words will often develop habits of producing non-functional memorized words/phrases to get caregivers to give them praise or treats. It is important for language facilitators to offer full-sentence language models to help facilitate integration of new vocabulary instead of memorization.

Level 04

Functional Needs-Based Speech

Late talkers use the memorized labels from the last level more consistently and accurately to share their needs with others. They will use memorized vocabulary along with their own tested 'phrases that work' to communicate with all of the different listeners in their environment. The late talker's typical requests are usually statements that combine the vocabulary they learned in different situations to describe the situations they want to manifest in the real world. '*I filled my cup, The water spilled. My shirt is wet. I need a new shirt.*'

The late talker starts to choose speech as the tool of choice as they share complex and specific information about their toys and experiences. It's common to hear the first basic sentence-level productions to describe scenes, solve problems, and respond to prompts and questions during test taking. The late talker will also be empowered to share details regarding what they do NOT like about their experiences. 'All done work time, I want swing.'

This is a common level of plateau, because the late talker is now more successful and uses words instead of behaviors most of the time. Facilitators and late talkers can fall into a comfort zone.

Levels of Functional Spoken Language Expression

Level 05

Social verbal expression to share ideas

At this level, the late talker becomes interested in verbal language expansion for sharing internal thoughts, ideas and opinions. You may hear phrases that the late talker has frequently heard other speakers using with good success to communicate their emotions and help others understand their problems. This is the stage where late talkers will 'pick up' swear words that are said during emotional outbursts or fun phrases that their teachers, peers, characters, or caregivers often say when they are trying to get attention and have fun. They can learn to answer common questions about themselves and their experiences. This level of expression is all about the late talker's evolving ability to share internal thoughts and feelings without behaviors. Language attempts evolve from descriptive sentences to connected dialogue for story telling and sharing drama.

At this stage late talkers can identify different languages and understand each speakers' unique characteristics. You may observe them trying to use matching communication styles with each communication partner as their way to enhance the ability for that person to understand them. Tantrums are limited to moments of communication breakdown which happens when the late talker is unable to access the vocabulary they need to accurately describe their wants, needs, or feelings.

Level 06

Expression of abilities / Negotiation for power

This is the level where late talkers show everyone who will listen that they WANT to be talkers. These late talkers know how to get attention from good language facilitators and Initiate conversation using words. These late talkers work hard to practice and produce their best speech with their best articulation because they know they are being judged and tested often. They can be taught to listen for their own (and others) speech accuracy, and can often be observed self correcting evolving skills.

Late talkers at this level can be self critical as a result of previous failures, and some may refuse to talk unless they feel safe to try without judgement. They have opinions about what is right for them and they will try to negotiate boundaries that feel too restrictive. Excited learners may be heard talking non-stop with a mix of ever-evolving vocabulary and phrases. They may be practicing talking with their reflection, toys, books, videos, or imaginary friends.

Levels of Functional Spoken Language Expression

Level 07

Confident using spoken language as a tool to expand their knowledge and share their wisdom with the world

At this point they can no longer be considered a late talker, because they have clearly caught up to others in their age group. Some speech articulation or grammatical issues may persist, however they do not interfere at all with their ability to communicate even complex thoughts and ideas. The speaker is confident in their spoken language ability, and feels equipped with their own unique self-developed speech style and ability.

At this level, the talker will begin to ask thoughtful questions about topics they are excited to learn about. They use their success to self-motivate to improve their own outcomes and will try to do their best to 'reach for the stars'. At this point they appreciate the effort they have put in so far to learn the spoken language and use it properly to communicate in real-life functional ways. The speaker still cares about doing their best to see the highest possible outcomes from their efforts.

Speakers at this stage appreciate the gift of being a late talker. All late talkers who receive active language facilitation coaching and guidance, ultimately end up with the gift of their unique experience. They were guided through the process of evolution from complete nonverbal communication to spoken language that can be understood by everyone they encounter.

Just like anyone who has overcome a struggles to achieve excellence, these special people have the ability to show empathy and willingness to look beyond limiting beliefs to understand the meanings behind others' nonverbal communication. Many previously late talkers choose to use their self-developed speech to help others through community service. They also may feel empowered to use their speech to support their passions and get a job, drive a car, or even create a business. They have built a life successfully challenging outdated ideas about speech delay and are now confident sharing their wisdom with the world.

Find Your Present Levels and Plan Your Approach

INTUITIVE ANALYSIS METHOD

01

Analyze The Whole Situation

Challenge yourself to analyze each communication situation objectively. Notice how everyone is ***FEELING, LISTENING, AND COMMUNICATING***. Your goal is watch for patterns of behavior (habits) that show the late talker is evolving in each of the focus areas.

02

Intuitively Rate Each Area

Consider **ALL** experiences you can remember from the week of activities. **Don't overthink your decision.** Late talkers can move up AND down on each scale. They may skip levels with high-impact or emotional experiences. Keep data pure by choosing the level that represents the abilities that you have **clearly** observed over **ONLY** the period of time you are analyzing.

Learn From Your Experience

03

Identify what has CHANGED in the late talker's experience as you compare each level to your last analysis. Note the opportunities and strategies that created the biggest impact in your in your profile sheets. Check your own mindset and perspective on the process.

Use Your Home Videos To Help You With Analysis

VIDEO RECORDING TIPS

1

Record videos using your phone so they are easy to access and view later. Turn on lights and limit background noise so you can see and hear all communication behaviors clearly.

2

Record typical communication opportunities that reflect the reality of your life both inside and outside of your home.

3

Ask another adult to record you interacting with the late talker while they are not aware so you can analyze your connection and see the results of your efforts.

Collect video of times when communication breaks down to uncover blockages and change your strategies for a different outcome.

5

Record the late talker interacting with others to analyze their independent ability to communicate as well as the other facilitator's response to their communication attempts.

Late Talker Profile

Example

Get to know the late talker so you can see the world through their eyes.

NAME / AGE -

FREQUENT REQUESTS:
Activity, food, characters, color, music, clothes etc.

Visit Papa working, go outside, vehicles, crackers with Nutella, snuggles

CURRENT FAVORITE - *go outside*

FRUSTRATIONS -
What triggers feelings of Boredom, restriction, overwhelm, anxiety, embarrassment, fear

Papa working behind closed doors, can't go outside, wants treats instead of healthy food

CURRENT ISSUES - *Tantrum when Papa goes to work*

CURIOSITIES
What Toys, actions, topics do they explore on their own?

Workers outside, songs with action, looking at self while jumping/moving

CURRENT FAVORITE - *Body parts songs and jumping/action*

COMFORTS:
Movement, sensory... What do they use for regulation and soothing?

Watches Papa and imitates whatever he does. Snuggle with Mommy at night.

CURRENT FAVORITE - *Papa wrestling and making up games*

ANALYSIS OF STARTING LEVELS

3	*Connection*
2	*Listening*
2	*Speaking*

OVERALL ATTITUDE ABOUT SPEECH

Willing to try some actions but not saying words. Listening better when he is in a good mood. Gets mad when I don't do or say the right thing.

Language Facilitator Profile

Find your happiest path.

Example

NAME / RELATIONSHIP TO THE LATE TALKER -

FREQUENT REQUESTS:
What do you need the late talker to do more independently to make life easier.

Stay inside until it is time to go out.
Let Papa work and play with Mama.
Eat food at mealtime.

CURRENT WISH - *Stay inside and leave Papa work without crying*

FRUSTRATIONS -
What triggers feelings of worry, restriction, overwhelm, anxiety, embarrassment, fear

Crying when Papa goes to work. Pulling my hair when he is mad. Running outside.

CURRENT ISSUES - *He is more interested in Papa than in me these days*

CURIOSITIES
What do you find easy to do and enjoy learning more about?

Singing together and getting him curious about helping me with my jobs while Papa is working.

CURRENT FAVORITE - *Finding a job that will help us connect*

COMFORTS:
Movement, sensory... What do YOU use for regulation and soothing?

Gratitude before bed reminds me of progress. I watch him while I drink chai and think about what he is thinking. Silly, fun, no-pressure snack time.

CURRENT FAVORITE - *I feel good when I see him happy and excited.*

ANALYSIS OF STARTING MINDSET

4 Mindset Level

Describe how you feel about your journey:

Encouraged by small changes and motivated to keep trying.

BIGGEST GOALS FOR YOUR JOURNEY

What do you intend to accomplish?

Better participating and longer attention for activities so I can talk more.
Get him motivated and relaxed about talking so he tries to say words.

SPOKEN LANGUAGE DEVELOPMENT **ANALYSIS/PLAN**

Based on review of language facilitation experiences for the week of:

Example A

▸ 1. [3] Level of connection, attention, and listening to language models
1-2 minutes max listening, only when I'm very animated and fun.

▸ 2. [2] Level of understanding and processing during language facilitation activities
Comes when I call him for going out. Calms easier when I explain.

▸ 3. [2] Level of using speech for primary expression
Pulling me, bringing shoes to go out, babbling 'word-like' speech

▸ 4. This week's 3 most successful language facilitation opportunities:
1- Swinging while I sing his favorite songs and talk about him.
2- Snuggling in bed and learning what our body parts are for.
3- Getting the mail - Teaching how to open the box, sort junk mail and delivering the important letters to Daddy.

▸ 5. Plan for Progress

Strategy to Maintain a Positive Language Facilitation Environment

Strategy to Connect in the LF Zone and Facilitate Attention and Listening

Strategy to Facilitate Understanding and Processing of Speech

Strategy to Motivate Increased Effort to Talk

Strategy Ideas are Found in Section 2

Language Facilitator Mindset Level [4]

▸ Child's Name: *Will B Talker*

▸ Facilitator/Analyst *Mama Talker*

SECTION

02

CREATE YOUR PLAN TO ELEVATE THE LEVELS

Once you analyze the late talker's current level in each of the areas, your job as facilitator is to connect the late talker and inspire them with FUN opportunities to TRY every day and rise up to the next level of spoken language naturally.

Functional spoken language emerges faster when ALL of the target areas are facilitated at the same time. This section will provide the resources necessary for you to create amazing language facilitation opportunities.

When they feel equipped and empowered with language models for the words THEY need, late talkers ALWAYS give up behaviors and start talking.

DECIDE HOW YOU WILL TAKE ACTION

RESOURCES FOR PLANNING

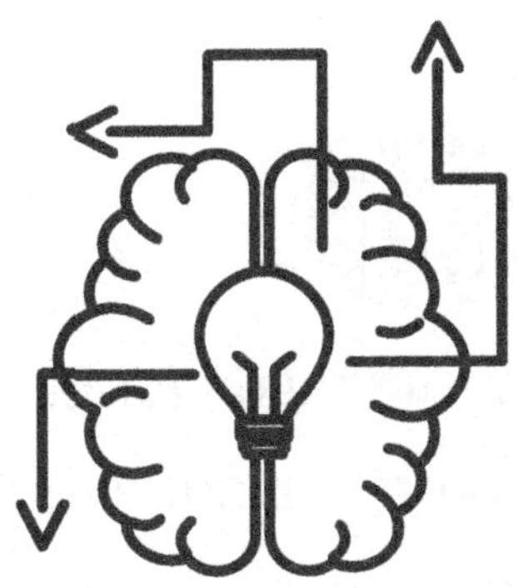

OPPORTUNITY CREATION FORMULA

The formula allows language facilitators to use your knowledge and connection with the late talker to create everyday opportunities for functional language facilitation. **Language learning is always a personal choice**, so the activities you design must be so attractive that the late talker will not be able to resist. Your opportunities will help speech learning seem easy, happy, safe, and FUN so progress happens without 'work'.

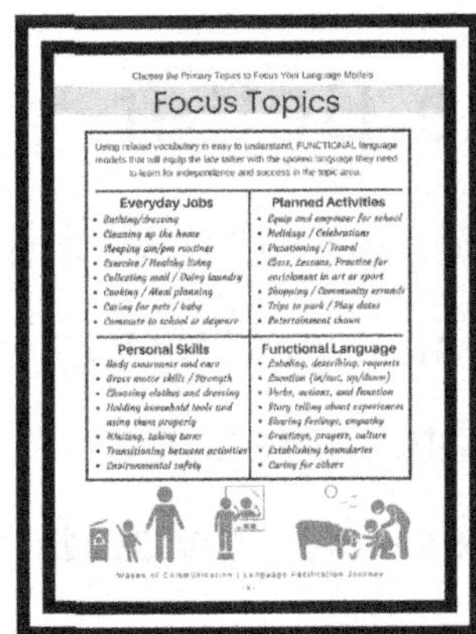

Choose the Primary Topics to Focus Your Language Models

Focus Topics

Using related vocabulary in easy to understand, FUNCTIONAL language models that will equip the late talker with the spoken language they need to learn for independence and success in the topic area.

Everyday Jobs	Planned Activities
• *Bathing/dressing* • *Cleaning up the home* • *Sleeping am/pm routines* • *Exercise / Healthy living* • *Collecting mail / Doing laundry* • *Cooking / Meal planning* • *Caring for pets / baby* • *Commute to school or daycare*	• *Equip and empower for school* • *Holidays / Celebrations* • *Vacationing / Travel* • *Class, Lessons, Practice for enrichment in art or sport* • *Shopping / Community errands* • *Trips to park / Play dates* • *Entertainment shows*
Personal Skills	**Functional Language**
• *Body awareness and care* • *Gross motor skills / Strength* • *Choosing clothes and dressing* • *Holding household tools and using them properly* • *Waiting, taking turns* • *Transitioning between activities* • *Environmental safety*	• *Labeling, describing, requests* • *Emotion (in/out, up/down)* • *Verbs, actions, and function* • *Story telling about experiences* • *Sharing feelings, empathy* • *Greetings, prayers, culture* • *Establishing boundaries* • *Caring for others*

Waves of Communication | Language Facilitation Journey

FOCUS TOPICS - WHAT TO TALK ABOUT

Language facilitation has the most impact when language models are provided in the moment during functional communication experiences. This page provides examples of the most effective situations that families are using worldwide to teach functional, topic-specific speech. Just one high-impact opportunity can facilitate real functional change in any of the areas of focus for spoken language success.

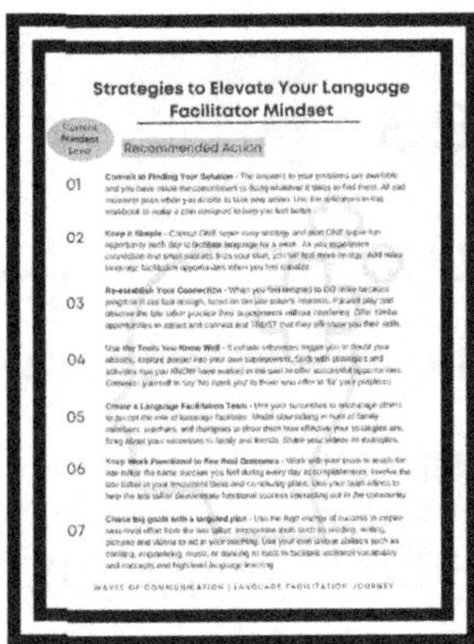

Strategies to Elevate Your Language Facilitator Mindset

Current Mindset Level — Recommended Action

01 **Commit to Finding Your Solution** - [illegible]

02 **Keep it Simple** - [illegible]

03 **Re-establish Your Connection** - [illegible]

04 **Use the Tools You Know Well** - [illegible]

05 **Create a Language Facilitation Team** - [illegible]

06 **Keep Work Functional to See Real Outcomes** - [illegible]

07 **Chase big goals with a targeted plan** - [illegible]

WAVES OF COMMUNICATION | LANGUAGE FACILITATION JOURNEY

STRATEGY INSPIRATION CHARTS

These charts provide strategies to create your language models. You will learn to use clear, effective demonstrations of the spoken language that the late talker needs to evolve their speech. The strategies are designed to help facilitate the next level of evolution and help you move through levels where you feel stuck. Each late talker will respond differently based on their physical well being, emotional mindset, and feeling of safety and empowerment in the environment.

CHOOSE IDEAS THAT SHOW POTENTIAL

OPPORTUNITY CREATION FORMULA

Choose a Focus Topic 01

What you say (your speech models) is the most important consideration for language facilitators. Consider the **functional jobs** and **planned activities** that are already on your schedule. What **personal skills** will equip and empower a greater level of success. Choose a **functional concept** and model it across many different activities.

02 Choose Skills That Make Life Better

Use your knowledge of previous experiences to select activities you KNOW the late talker cares about. Your goal is to create opportunities that always FEEL motivating, easy, safe, and FUN - never pressured or desperate for results. Encourage participation and imitation by making the activity feel like play and abandoning your expectations and comparisons. Trust the late talker is trying their best and celebrate every EFFORT. Remember to ENJOY the connection you feel.

Choose Repeatable Strategies 03

Use the charts to find ONE strategy in each area to elevate the late talker's ability to the next level. The strategy you select should seem easy enough for you to do 2-3 hours every day. Use the strategies to craft your language models for a whole new way of talking that the late talker is sure to notice and respond to. Watch for increased attention and focus as you consistently model the spoken language for the thoughts and ideas THEY want to talk about.

Focus Topics

Using related vocabulary in easy to understand, FUNCTIONAL language models that will equip the late talker with the spoken language they need to learn for independence and success in the topic area.

Everyday Jobs

- *Bathing/dressing*
- *Cleaning up the home*
- *Sleeping am/pm routines*
- *Exercise / Healthy living*
- *Collecting mail / Doing laundry*
- *Cooking / Meal planning*
- *Caring for pets / baby*
- *Commute to school or daycare*

Planned Activities

- *Equip and empower for school*
- *Holidays / Celebrations*
- *Vacationing / Travel*
- *Class, Lessons, Practice for enrichment in art or sport*
- *Shopping / Community errands*
- *Trips to park / Play dates*
- *Entertainment shows*

Personal Skills

- *Body awareness and care*
- *Gross motor skills / Strength*
- *Choosing clothes and dressing*
- *Holding household tools and using them properly*
- *Waiting, taking turns*
- *Transitioning between activities*
- *Environmental safety*

Functional Language

- *Labeling, describing, requests*
- *Location (in/out, up/down)*
- *Verbs, actions, and function*
- *Story telling about experiences*
- *Sharing feelings, empathy*
- *Greetings, prayers, culture*
- *Establishing boundaries*
- *Caring for others*

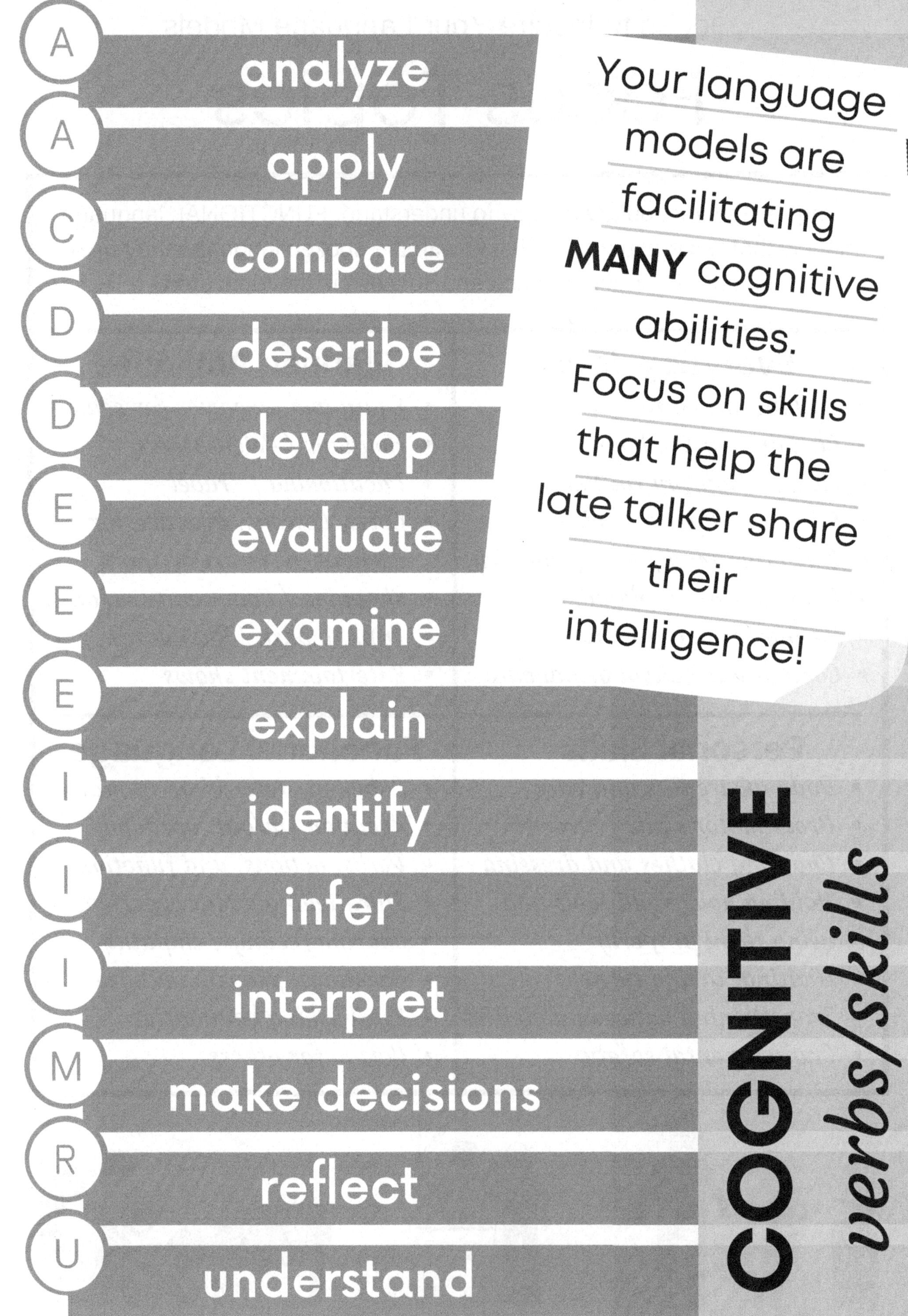
A
analyze
A
apply
C
compare
D
describe
D
develop
E
evaluate
E
examine
E
explain
I
identify
I
infer
I
interpret
M
make decisions
R
reflect
U
understand
Your language models are facilitating **MANY** cognitive abilities. Focus on skills that help the late talker share their intelligence!
COGNITIVE
verbs/skills

Strategies to Elevate Your Language Facilitator Mindset

Current **Mindset** Level

Recommended Action

01 **Commit to Finding Your Solution -** The answers to your problems are available and you have made the commitment to doing whatever it takes to find them. All sad moments pass when you decide to take new action. Use the resources in this workbook to make a plan designed to help you feel better.

02 **Keep it Simple -** Choose ONE super-easy strategy and plan ONE super-fun opportunity each day to facilitate language for a week. As you experience connection and small success from your start, you will find more energy. Add more language facilitation opportunities when you feel capable.

03 **Re-establish Your Connection -** When you feel tempted to DO more because progress is not fast enough, focus on the late talker's interests. Parallel play and observe the late talker practice their superpowers without interfering. Offer similar opportunities to attract and connect and TRUST that they will show you their skills.

04 **Use the Tools You Know Well -** If outside influences trigger you to doubt your abilities, explore deeper into your own superpowers. Stick with strategies and activities that you KNOW have worked in the past to offer successful opportunities. Empower yourself to say 'No thank you' to those who offer to 'fix' your problems.

05 **Create a Language Facilitation Team -** Use your successes to encourage others to accept the role of language facilitator. Model slow talking in front of family members, teachers, and therapists to show them how effective your strategies are. Brag about your successes to family and friends. Share your videos as examples.

06 **Keep Work Functional to See Real Outcomes -** Work with your team to teach the late talker the same success you feel during every day accomplishments. Involve the late talker in your household tasks and community plans. Use your team efforts to help the late talker demonstrate functional success interacting out in the community.

07 **Chase big goals with a targeted plan -** Use the high energy of success to inspire next-level effort from the late talker. Incorporate tools such as reading, writing, pictures and videos to aid in your teaching. Use your own unique abilities such as cooking, engineering, music, or dancing as tools to facilitate technical vocabulary and concepts and high level language learning.

To Facilitate Connection in the LF Zone

Inspire Curiosity About Speech

Current **Connection** Level

Recommended Action

01 Stop intervention and hold space by offering open arms at the late talker's eye level, acknowledge the fear they feel and offer a safe place where only understanding and comfort is provided. 'Wait a minute...You are really upset, I'll help you feel better. I know you have a problem. Let's figure this out together.'

02 Demonstrate how useful, and EASY spoken language learning is by talking very slowly using FUN phrases. Focus on being attractive and enticing curiosity to watch and learn from your examples. Remind the late talker that you have zero expectation of performance. '*Watch me, it's easy! You can try when you are ready.*'

03 Talk specifically about the late talker's struggles (drama) and respond to their needs so they know you understand their frustration. 'You are not happy sitting here. You can listen better when you are swinging, let's go to the park.' Remind the late talker of their superpowers. 'You have a great memory! You helped me find my keys!

04 Provide more teaching than testing. Replace questions with statements and demonstrate every step of multi-step skills slowly. Encourage participation without any demands. 'You don't water, you want chocolate milk. OK, That's a good idea. Let's get what we need and make it together. First let's get a glass.'

05 Reach into the late talker's comfort zone and join them with their favorite activities to remind them that their unique ideas and fun are also valuable to you. Remind them that you are interested in helping them explore and elevate their interests to new levels. '*Can I watch with you? Wow, that dinosaur is powerful. This feels exciting!*'

06 Introduce fun challenges to elevate excitement and offer opportunities to practice focused effort, reach beyond their comfort zone, and work hard to reach for new goals. '*Thanks for helping me cook. I'm very excited to taste the chicken you made. It's time to invite Dad to eat the dinner. Remind him to wash his hands.*'

07 Turn obsession into function by offering coaching opportunities. Maintain high motivation for ongoing improvement by showing appreciation for the late talker's efforts. 'You are trying so hard to say all of the sounds. I hear you talking better every day. I love your ideas! What do you think about this? You are so smart!'

To Facilitate Attention and Listening

Demonstrate Functional Speech

Current **Listening** Level

Recommended Action

01 Attention is fleeting so use visual cues and voice changes to be super attractive. Hold toys and objects by your face and look into mirrors together as you talk. Repeat phrases and re-introduce situations frequently so the late talker can start to make first associations and memorize labels for objects and activities important to them.

02 Introduce new vocabulary concepts during activities. Use many visual aids to help the late talker understand ideas they have never even conceived of. The goal is to increase attention as you spark curiosity. Talk in complete sentences and describe how you feel to associate words with feelings. '*This food makes my tummy happy.*'

03 Introduce vocabulary through experiences. Model labels and concepts in expanded sentences with varied examples. Focus on the concept's functional applications. *'Look at that cute dog. This dog is black and that dog is brown. Our dog Rex is big and fluffy. That small dog is jumping. Dogs say woof. She is afraid of dogs.'*

04 Provide more teaching than testing. Replace questions with statements and demonstrate every step of multi-step skills slowly. Encourage participation without any demands. 'You don't water, you want chocolate milk. OK, That's a good idea. Let's get what we need and make it together. First let's get a glass.'

05 Choose a daily situation and model the speech and action you want to see. Model phrases with visual cues to help the late talker understand WHY and HOW things happen in your environment. 'You want me to hurry because your tummy is hungry. I will work super fast to make your food. Watch me, I'm getting my pan and cooking.'

06 Talk SLOWLY using kid-friendly phrases that are easy and fun to say. Use familiar words in new ways to expand sentences. Emphasize words and sounds that the late talker is still working on learning how to say correctly. Use pretend play opportunities to demonstrate and role-play the communication situation from all perspectives.

07 Tell stories about the late talker's life with the people they encounter every day. Look at or create pictures and videos of your experiences or make up stories to share imagination. Show how to appreciate the lessons you learn and show emapthy for others who are learning from their own trials and errors.

To Facilitate Effort to Improve Speech

Model Speech the Late Talker Needs

Current **Speaking** Level

Recommended Action

01 Big emotions and movement neurologically trigger both listening and subconscious speech tries. Model fun expressions during play. Incorporate movement on swings/jumping/running to encourage speech that could pop out naturally. 'Wow, We did it, Uh Oh, Whee, Bummer, That was hard.'

02 Model super useful phrases that help show the late talker how easy it is to get attention and direct others. 'Come with me, I need help, Open this, I can't reach, more please, all done, no thank you.' Talk about your own feelings to model helpful vocabulary. 'I'm excited to run, That's so pretty! Ice cream makes my tummy happy.'

03 Model phrases for requesting functionally and describe what you will do to meet demands. 'You need help. You want Mom to open this. It is stuck and you can't get what is inside. OK I will use my muscles and twist it. UHG! Yay! I did it.' Share opinions and fun details that the late talker will appreciate. 'That poop is stinky,

04 Provide more teaching than testing. Replace questions with statements and demonstrate every step of multi-step skills slowly. Encourage participation without any demands. 'You don't water, you want chocolate milk. OK, That's a good idea. Let's get what we need and make it together. First let's get a glass.'

05 Use SLOW clear, easy-to-try phrases with encouragement to imitate. Respond to incorrect speech attempts with acknowledgement of effort and 'recast' of the late talker's idea using the correct speech to model how it should sound. 'You said mom, look at my BLocK Tower. Your block tower is so cool. GREAT talking!'

06 Equip the late talker with a fun environment to explore and take risks with spoken language expression. Encourage creativity through pretend play stories. Empower the late talker to share their wisdom. Put on a show in the living room, ask them to show you what they are playing or share it with family members and peers.

07 Use your experience together to remind the late talker about the lessons they have learned and how their new strategies that have worked well to help them get this far with speech. Offer daily opportunities to have conversation and practice and using spoken language to connect in the language facilitation zone to share ideas.

SPOKEN LANGUAGE DEVELOPMENT **ANALYSIS/PLAN**

Example B

Based on review of language facilitation experiences for the week of:

21 - 27 November, 2021

▶ 1. [3] Level of connection, attention, and listening to language models

1-2 minutes max listening, only when I'm very animated and fun.

▶ 2. [2] Level of understanding and processing during language facilitation activities

Comes when I call him for fun activities. Calms easier.

▶ 3. [2] Level of using speech for primary expression

Pulling me, bringing shoes to go out, babbling 'word-like' speech

▶ 4. This week's 3 most successful language facilitation opportunities:

1- Swinging while I sing his favorite songs and talk about him.

2- Snuggling in bed and learning what our body parts are for.

3- Getting the mail - Teaching how to open the box, sort junk mail and delivering the important letters to Daddy.

▶ 5. Plan for Progress

Strategy to Maintain a Positive Language Facilitation Environment

Every morning Papa will remind him that he is learning to talk better and every evening I will remind him about all of his effort.

Strategy to Connect in the LF Zone and Facilitate Attention and Listening

Concentrate on talking slow and saying full sentences to expand words that he knows without expecting any imitation.

Strategy to Facilitate Understanding and Processing of Speech

Focus on VERBS to talk about the actions and purposes of every NOUN we see. Use verbs to talk the actions we do and see in others.

Strategy to Motivate Increased Effort to Talk

Papa will model easy phrases during play. Practice jobs repeatedly and celebrate his effort by describing his actions.

Language Facilitator Mindset Level [4]

▶ Child's Name: *Will B Talker*

▶ Facilitator/Analyst *Mama Talker*

SECTION

03

WORK YOUR PLAN

Implement Strategies Every Day
Journal / Collect Data

This section will help you get organized and use what you have learned to create a language facilitation system that you can repeat every day and stay with consistently for LONG TERM action and ultimate success.

You will learn how to use your journal to collect data to show how your efforts are resulting in functional spoken language improvement. This step is important to identify blockages in your process and know when it is time to elevate your language facilitation strategies.

RESOURCES FOR FOCUSED ACTION

WEEKLY ITINERARY

WEEKLY ITINERARY

This tool helps you to plan 4 activities for every day as your foundation for all-day language facilitation. As you go through the week, you will be able to record important opportunities that pop up naturally. You can also record events such as new words or big emotional triggers. The itinerary also allows you to think about scheduled events of the next few weeks as you teach functional skills to prepare the late talker for success everywhere you go.

DAILY RECORD

DAILY RECORD

This form allows you to record your data. At the end of each day, you can analyze your results and assign levels for all of the areas. Over the week, you will create a document that reports a clear picture of your experience. It is important to remain objective and provide details about your experiences so you can notice the habits and patterns of behavior that create progress or block it. Your daily record keeping will help you stay consistent and hold yourself accountable for daily action.

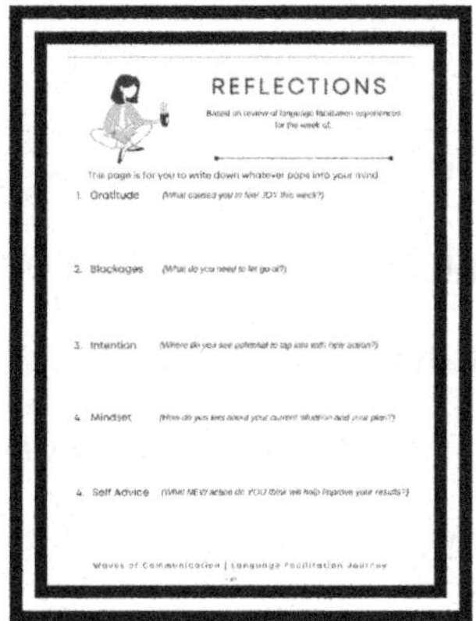
REFLECTIONS

WEEKLY JOURNAL EXPERIENCE

This page is where you record your experience as you evolve habits and patterns that turn you into a full-time language facilitator. This journal page will serve as a diary to reflect and share how your experience changes you personally, from the inside out. You will learn how to tap into the 'best version of yourself' and bring it forward every day to share with the world. Your results will soar as you become an unstoppable language facilitator realizing your true power lies when you remain conscious, connected, grateful, and HAPPY.

Your Guide to Daily Action

WEEKLY ITINERARY TIPS

01 Think Like the Late Talker

Language facilitation happens best when you are connected in the moment. Late talkers have short attention for anything that they do not BELIEVE is not useful or FUN. Not all of your opportunities will hit the mark. Follow the late talker's lead. Abandon ideas that are (repeatedly) ignored or refused and repeat those experiences that they love, especially if they ask for them. Remember the late talker is YOUR audience, depending on YOU to provide language models that they like, support their efforts with coaching, and be their cheerleader for EVERY effort, no matter how small.

02 Flexible and Open-Minded

Stay Present. You never know when the next language facilitation opportunity will happen. Every new situation you introduce has the potential to teach. One key to maximizing your language facilitation time is to be aware of emotional triggers. When you or the late talker have BIG feelings, instead of reacting, you can use the moment to show how spoken language is the best way to respond to unexpected or unwanted influences and learn from every trial **and** error.

Be Brave. Instead of avoiding situations that have historically been challenging, such as parties or religious services, use the opportunity to coach the late talker to develop the skills they need to be successful, such as waiting and respecting the quiet spaces. Incorporate the late talker in the planning, preparation, and clean-up of every opportunity you are offering as a way to maintain more time in the language facilitation zone and expand your teaching of functional concepts and abilities. Teach them to use tools and navigate risks consciously like big kids do.

WEEKLY ITINERARY

Language Facilitation Opportunities

Topic(s) of Focus: *Body parts, asking for food, scooter riding, getting mail*

For the Week of: ***Example***

	MORNING	MID- DAY	EVENING	MEALTIME
MONDAY	*Body parts in bed at wake up*	*Walk around the block -Dogs*	*Body parts at bath time*	*Requesting food at dinner*
TUESDAY	*Body parts in bed at wake up*	*Swinging and singing at park*	*in/out with mailbox*	*Cutting fruits for snack*
WEDNESDAY	*Body parts in bed at wake up*	*Meet friends at the park*	*Get the mail deliver letters*	*Requesting food at dinner*
THURSDAY	*Body parts in bed at wake up*	*Cleaning up the house*	*in/out movie about mail*	*Requesting water and snack*
FRIDAY	*Body parts in bed at wake up*	*Scooter in the house*	*Get the mail deliver letters*	*Using the Tap clean up mess*
SATURDAY	*Body parts in bed at wake up*	*Scooter play at park*	*in/out with junk mail in the trash*	*Requesting food at dinner*
SUNDAY	*Body parts in bed at wake up*	*Scooter play at park*	*Get the mail deliver letters*	*Requesting food at dinner*

UPCOMING EVENTS TO PLAN FOR:

Family birthday party next week

Doctor visit with shots in 2 weeks *Bike/scooter playdate??*

IMPORTANT OPPORTUNITIES OF THE WEEK:

Scooter and swinging got the most eye contact and listening

He touches the body part when I sing and label 10-15 different ones.

He said 'na' for banana and 'wa' for water right after he was eating or drinking

I was triggered by my friend talking about therapy and didn't talk much that day.

Getting the mail is his new favorite job. Daddy is playing along very well.

Your Data Collection Tool

DAILY RECORD FORM

Collect useful data

Language facilitation is an intuitive process. You will be using your own observations and reflections of the entire communication situation to determine what is important for you to document. There is no need for testing when you are present and pay attention to communication habits, patterns, and functional speech as it evolves.

- Document **NEW communication behaviors** you observe to indicate a change is happening
- Document communication **observed on a consistent basis** to indicate that the late talker has reached a new level.

Analyze the environment to identify blockages

Spoken language development is not a linear process. Every day will be filled with different experiences that cause the levels to move up and down. High-impact experiences create BIG changes, because learning happens fast with the focus that is required to maintain both connection and effort with high-level energy.

Always evaluate experiences from the perspective of the late talker to identify what is **motivating them to try harder** and what **turns them off of listening**. Experiences where the late talker feels judgement and pressure adds a layer of anxiety into the process that blocks learning. When you see what triggers anxiety, you will learn what you need to change in your approach, or assist the late talker with training and support to facilitate tolerance and acceptance of experiences that are not fun.

Focus your attention on behaviors that show the late talker is TRYING to make progress. As soon as a late talker experiences success with a spoken language concept functionally, they will continue to practice it and elevate it as long as you keep on facilitating fun opportunities.

DAILY RECORD

Dates: **Example**

Topic(s) of Focus: *Body parts, asking for food, scooter riding, mail collecting*

C=Connection / L=Listening / S = Speaking / M = Language Facilitator Mindset

Day	C	L	S	M	Observations
MON	5	5	4	6	*Morning snuggles in bed was a hit! He loves when I talk slow. Today was patient and stopped myself from prompting to follow his lead.*
TUE	5	5	4	6	*The swing was his favorite activity. He watched when I showed him how to cut a banana and tried it on his own. He said 'na' for banana.*
WED	4	4	4	3	*Went out and he was a little anxious. Family friend saw him flapping and made a comment about calling a therapist. He did not do his best.*
THU	5	5	4	4	*Quiet day. He brought me his cup to ask for water. I showed him how to turn on the tap and he imitated 'wa' for water after he took a drink.*
FRI	6	5	4	5	*Saw kids on bikes and found his scooter. I was able to help him understand about wearing the helmet. No talking today, but making noises.*
SAT	6	5	4	6	*Took scooter to park and he loved practicing. We talked about going slow and watching out for holes and bumps. He followed every direction!*
SUN	6	6	4	6	*Watched videos of his scooter riding and talked about his progress. He was listening and said his name when he saw himself on the screen.*

What Changed This Week?

- *When I talked slowly I got better listening and eye contact.*
- *I was able to talk through tantrums and calm him down more easily.*
- *He has a new interest in bikes after he saw some kids riding.*
- *The mail job is going well and Daddy is playing along.*

Keeping a Record of **Your** Experience

JOURNALING TIPS

Trust **Your** Plan Above All Others

01

Your life experiences with the late talker put you in the best position to create opportunities that will resonate with the special soul you are here to help. You know best what life goals you have for their future and you will be naturally inspired to take the action that feels like it is taking you in the right direction. The charts and examples should serve as inspiration for your own creativity. Don't be afraid to follow your gut.

02

Know You are **Destined For Success**

You were given the opportunity to facilitate language for this child and you know them best. You are also trying your best every day. Be on the lookout for signs that you are making progress. When you see better eye contact or hear beginning speech pop out, BELIEVE that this 'data' that proves your strategies are working. Speech is not usually perfect when it first emerges and you don't want miss any effort that you can quickly facilitate into more evolved spoken language.

01

Appreciate Your Happy Reality **NOW**

You have taken on the **BEST job ever**. Overcoming challenges and reaching new levels in our natural talents and abilities (a.k.a. superpowers) is great FUN. These tools will help you create super-fun experiences every day. Consider every activity with wonder and curiosity. ***ACT like you KNOW the late talker will start talking*** because you are on the job. When you demonstrate their favorite speech EVERY DAY, the late talker will notice right away and want to join you. Speech always comes faster when the language facilitator is happy. **If it isn't FUN - it ISN'T fun.**

REFLECTIONS

Based on review of language facilitation experiences for the week of:

Example

This page is for you to write down whatever pops into your mind.

1. **Gratitude** *(What caused you to feel JOY this week?)*

Reflect on the moments that reminded you why you chose to take this language facilitation journey.

2. **Blockages** *(What do you need to let go of?)*

Reflect on internal or external triggers that caused you to feel low AND why you gave your power away to them.

3. **Intention** *(Where do you see potential to tap into with new action?)*

Reflect on the most successful activities you tried and decide how to repeat and evolve them.

4. **Mindset** *(How do you feel about your current situation and your plan?)*

Reflect on your overall energy and feelings of motivation to stay focused on your own action every day.

4. **Self Advice** *(What NEW action do YOU think will help improve your results?)*

Reflect on the guidance that you would recommend to another language facilitator who is in your postion.

SECTION

04

LEVEL UP YOUR OUTCOMES

This section has tools that will help you maximize your everyday action through elevated strategies that take your language facilitation outcomes to the next level.

Managing Your Triggers
Using Community Resources
Working With Your Energy
Continue Independent Learning
Experience Coaching

MANAGE YOUR TRIGGERS

Spot the signs you are triggered and turn your energy around

Your mental blockages and emotional triggers will take you off of your path fast. You created these triggers and you have the power to turn your mindset around instantly as long as you stay present and conscious, and response - ABLE.

Worry

Focus on NOW and Teach the skills you feel the late talker is lacking and needs for the future.

Comparison

Proudly reflect on your own accomplishments. Focus on the late talkers superpowers.

Prompting

Replace questions and directions with the answers and solutions. Say words the late talker wants to hear.

Fast/Loud Talking

Establish connection before you speak. Use attractive, SLOW speech to gain and keep attention.

Complaining

Appreciate your connection and the late talkers messages. Stick with on EASY and FUN activities.

Seeking Remedies

Connect with the late talker for ideas and inspiration. TRUST that YOUR process IS WORKING.

Facilitate A Variety of Language Models

COMMUNITY RESOURCES

ORGANIZE PLAY DATES

Neighbors, family members, and friends from church or class are the perfect peers to invite over. Simply include them in your opportunities and encourage them to provide their own unique language models too.

VISIT ATTRACTIONS

Attractions are designed for language facilitation! Zoos, aquariums, gardens, temples, museums, and such are perfect opportunities you can plan for, travel to, and navigate through. They usually are super attractive and offer ideas that will inspire you to teach as you explore. Follow the late talker's lead to see what aspects they are most interested in learning about.

USE PUBLIC TRANSPORT

This tool incorporates both movement and fun. Teach about the vehicles and their functions. Practice purchasing tickets. Connect with passengers and workers.

GO SHOPPING

- Shopping is a great time to teach boundaries and limits.
- Prepare your list by talking about the items in your home that are running out or empty.
- Explore the store to hunt for the items on your list.
- Compare items and discuss why you make your choices.
- Use other customers as your example to show how they are successfully shopping.
- Greet the cashier and talk about your shopping experience.
- Teach about payment methods.

GET OUTSIDE AND PLAY

- Chalk, Water play
- Running around / walks
- Playground equipment
- Bike, Skate, Scooter, Jump
- Dig in dirt or sand
- Hike and explore nature

Work With the Energy of the Chakras

Each chakra is color-coded to help align in the physical energy system. When inspired by a color in your environment or physical sensation in your body, use the strategies described below to understand a whole new level of facilitating spoken language development. The definitions move top to bottom.

- **Crown Chakra (Indigo)** - Late talkers develop a 'telepathic' connection with those who care for them as a way to help them communicate their basic needs easily without speech. This connection starts before birth and is what some call 'mother's intuition'. Language facilitators activate this area and use your connection to bring communication into the 3D world through your speech models.

- **Third Eye Chakra (Purple)** - Spoken language development happens when late talkers are motivated to share what they are thinking about with the people around them. Language facilitators use your intuition to connect and understand the intuitive messages behind the 'low-level' communication behaviors you are seeing with your actual eyes. Imagine 'high level' ideas the late talker is thinking and translate what you 'perceive' into speech. Activate this area by reviewing family images and discussing your mutual experiences.

- **Throat Chakra (Blue)** - ALL humans have this special energy spot specifically designed to fuel our ability to use spoken language as a way to communicate and connect with others. Late talkers who experience fear surrounding their efforts at speech need language facilitators to help them realize that talking is easy, happy, safe, and FUN. Your 'language facilitation talk' will be the key to eliminating fear and activating this ultra-important energy for spoken language development.

- **Heart Chakra (Green)** - This is the area where we feel the language facilitation zone connection. The heart center is the 'second brain' of the energy system where feelings and emotions are processed. Loving words of appreciation, empathy, and empowerment activate the heart chakra. This area is often closed off intentionally by late talkers who feel judged or pressured to do things they don't enjoy.

- **Solar Plexus Chakra (Yellow)** - Late talkers need to feel a sense of control in their world so they can confidently communicate their God-given abilities and wisdom out into the world. Language facilitators balance power in teaching and encourage freedom to express the unique ideas hiding inside. Offer lots of opportunity to practice natural talent as a way to activate this area.

- **Sacral Chakra (Orange)** - Late talkers become highly motivated to participate in learning and try your speech models for themselves when they are encouraged to access their natural creative energy. FUN activities inspire creative ways to motivate problem solving and teamwork. Pretend play, art projects, and music activate this area and provide many amazing opportunities to teach.

- **Root Chakra (Red)** - Late talkers can focus and learn only when they feel safe and fully equipped to rise to the challenges before them. Language facilitators empower late talkers so they can feel safe taking the risk of trying a whole new communication system. Dancing, running, climbing, and taking calculated risks like jumping from high places are great activities to activate the root chakra.

Learn More About Language Facilitation

CONTINUE LEARNING

Take Marci's Independent Study Course
Language Facilitation Basics
8 phases of learning via slideshow video presentations, with worksheets.

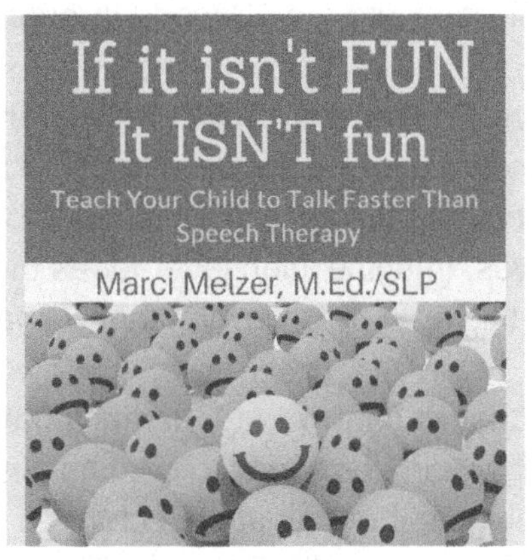

Read Marci's Book, If it isn't FUN It ISN'T fun - Teach Your Child to Talk Faster Than Speech Therapy is available on Amazon, Kindle, and Audible.

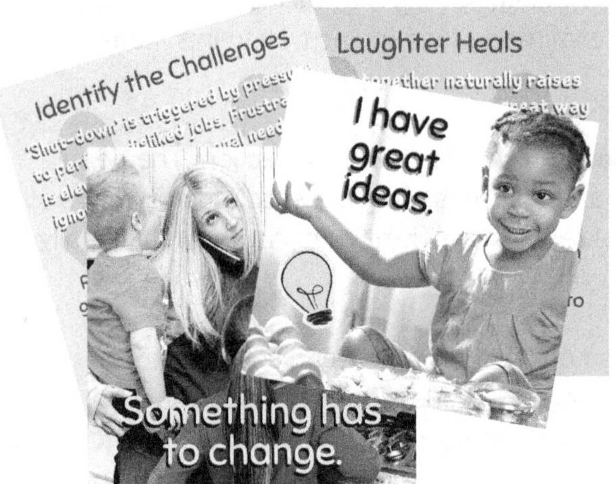

Try Marci's
Language Facilitation Inspiration Cards
71 images of Typical Situations
Practical Strategies
16 Page E-Guidebook with games and activities you can use by yourself, with the late talker, and other facilitators in your circle of influence.

Marci has produced more than 400 videos on YouTube with information, discussion, strategies, and step-by-step processes for all parents and caregivers to access.

Visit WavesofCommunication.com to learn more about resources

Gain Confidence and Achieve Your Ultimate Goals

EXPERIENCE COACHING

Join LIVE Q&A on YouTube

Marci produces a new coaching video every week and presents the information LIVE on YouTube and Facebook @ 11:00 am Eastern time US/New York on the Waves of Communication YouTube Channel. **You are welcome to post your questions and comments LIVE during the broadcast or leave it in the comments of the replay.**

Rocket Fuel for Your Journey

WOC Starter Coaching Program

- Comprehensive video analysis of your family communication
- Written report identifying all blockages you need to correct and strategies you need to incorporate.
- Meet with Marci in THREE, 2- hour recorded video calls spread out over your 11-week journey
- Guidance to establish and maintain your daily plan
- Support to help you firmly establish your language facilitation habits, overcome challenges, and maintain a positive mindset

WOC Lifetime Community Coaching Program

- Everything in the starter program and more
- Unlimited video analysis and email support
- Opportunity every week to join Marci personally for 1:1 coaching about any topic or issue that comes up
- Assistance as you navigate therapies, schools, etc.
- Mindset and energy work guidance for overall wellness
- A global community of language facilitators to connect with

Visit WavesofCommunication.com to learn about coaching options

SECTION

05

YOUR JOURNAL

This section is where you will record your experience.

Profile Sheets
Analysis / Plan Form
Weekly Itinerary
Daily Record
Reflections Journal Entry

Journal Documents

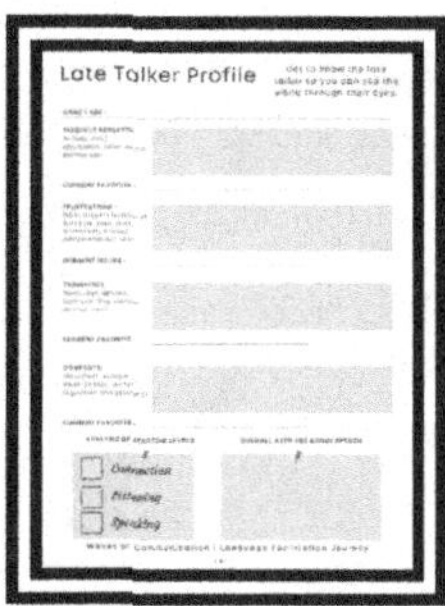

Profile Sheets

Complete this analysis every few weeks as it appears along your language facilitation journal documents. Update the info to provide a 'big picture' analysis of current trends that have contributed to all of your current levels. Use the info to keep your topics and activities current, attractive, and always evolving.

Analysis / Plan Form

Complete this form at the beginning of the week. Use the information from your analysis and the strategies charts to create an ever-evolving plan. This form provides a snapshot of the current skills and abilities that are active and evolving in the language facilitation environment.

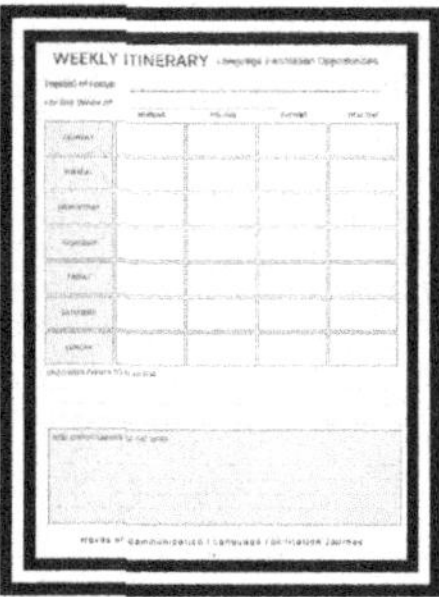

Weekly Itinerary

Complete this form every week after you finish your Analysis/Plan. Review it at the beginning of your day and make changes as necessary. Share the day's itinerary with the late talker and make notes about observations and ideas you want to keep track of.

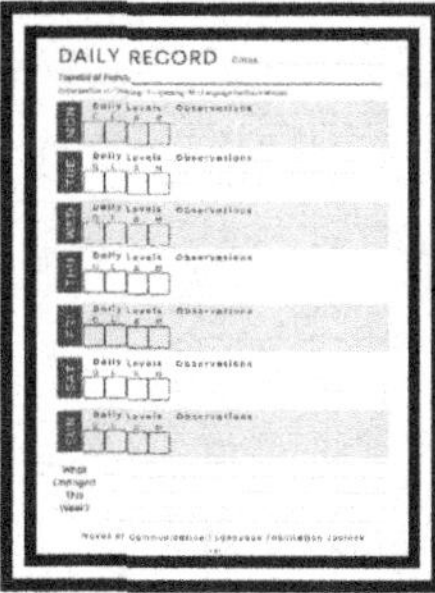

Daily Record

Complete this form every day at the end of the day. Complete the summary portion at the end of the week. This will be your record of data to use for your next week's Analysis/Plan form and Weekly Itinerary.

Reflection Journal Page

Add to this page any time you feel inspired, and always at the end of the week. Complete your reflection BEFORE you move on to the next week's records. Your reflections about your efforts and results will provide inspiration and motivation to continue on your journey with maximum power and efficiency.

Late Talker Profile

Get to know the late talker so you can see the world through their eyes.

NAME / AGE -

FREQUENT REQUESTS:
Activity, food, characters, color, music, clothes etc.

CURRENT FAVORITE -

FRUSTRATIONS -
What triggers feelings of Boredom, restriction, overwhelm, anxiety, embarrassment, fear

CURRENT ISSUES -

CURIOSITIES
What Toys, actions, topics do they explore on their own?

CURRENT FAVORITE -

COMFORTS:
Movement, sensory... What do they use for regulation and soothing?

CURRENT FAVORITE -

ANALYSIS OF STARTING LEVELS

- [ ] *Connection*
- [ ] *Listening*
- [ ] *Speaking*

OVERALL ATTITUDE ABOUT SPEECH

Language Facilitator Profile

Find your happiest path.

NAME / RELATIONSHIP TO THE LATE TALKER -

FREQUENT REQUESTS:
What do you need the late talker to do more independently to make life easier.

CURRENT WISH -

FRUSTRATIONS -
What triggers feelings of worry, restriction, overwhelm, anxiety, embarrassment, fear

CURRENT ISSUES -

CURIOSITIES
What do you find easy to do and enjoy learning more about?

CURRENT FAVORITE -

COMFORTS:
Movement, sensory...
What do YOU use for regulation and soothing?

CURRENT FAVORITE -

ANALYSIS OF STARTING MINDSET

☐ Mindset Level

Describe how you feel about your journey:

BIGGEST GOALS FOR YOUR JOURNEY

What do you intend to accomplish?

SPOKEN LANGUAGE DEVELOPMENT **ANALYSIS/PLAN**

Based on review of language facilitation experiences for the week of:

▶ 1. ☐ Level of connection, attention, and listening to language models

▶ 2. ☐ Level of understanding and processing during language facilitation activities

▶ 3. ☐ Level of using speech for primary expression

This week's 3 most successful language facilitation opportunities:

▶ 4.

Plan for Progress

▶ 5.

Language Facilitator Mindset Level ☐

Strategy to Maintain a Positive Language Facilitation Environment

Strategy to Connect in the LF Zone and Facilitate Attention and Listening

Strategy to Facilitate Understanding and Processing of Speech

Strategy to Motivate Increased Effort to Talk

▶ Child's Name:

▶ Facilitator/Analyst

WEEKLY ITINERARY Language Facilitation Opportunities

Topic(s) of Focus: ______________________

For the Week of: ______________________

	MORNING	MID- DAY	EVENING	MEALTIME
MONDAY				
TUESDAY				
WEDNESDAY				
THURSDAY				
FRIDAY				
SATURDAY				
SUNDAY				

UPCOMING EVENTS TO PLAN FOR:

BEST OPPORTUNITIES OF THE WEEK:

DAILY RECORD

Dates:

Topic(s) of Focus:

C=Connection / L=Listening / S = Speaking / M = Language Facilitator Mindset

MON

Daily Levels — C L S M

Observations

TUE

Daily Levels — C L S M

Observations

WED

Daily Levels — C L S M

Observations

THU

Daily Levels — C L S M

Observations

FRI

Daily Levels — C L S M

Observations

SAT

Daily Levels — C L S M

Observations

SUN

Daily Levels — C L S M

Observations

What Changed This Week?

REFLECTIONS

Based on review of language facilitation experiences
for the week of:

This page is for you to write down whatever pops into your mind.

1. **Gratitude** *(What caused you to feel JOY this week?)*

2. **Blockages** *(What do you need to let go of?)*

3. **Intention** *(Where do you see potential to tap into with new action?)*

4. **Mindset** *(How do you feel about your current situation and your plan?)*

4. **Self Advice** *(What NEW action do YOU think will help improve your results?)*

SPOKEN LANGUAGE DEVELOPMENT **ANALYSIS/PLAN**

Based on review of language facilitation experiences for the week of:

____

▸ 1.	☐ Level of connection, attention, and listening to language models
▸ 2.	☐ Level of understanding and processing during language facilitation activities
▸ 3.	☐ Level of using speech for primary expression

This week's 3 most successful language facilitation opportunities:

▸ 4.

Plan for Progress

▸ 5.

Strategy to Maintain a Positive Language Facilitation Environment

Strategy to Connect in the LF Zone and Facilitate Attention and Listening

Strategy to Facilitate Understanding and Processing of Speech

Strategy to Motivate Increased Effort to Talk

Language Facilitator Mindset Level ☐

▸ Child's Name: ....

▸ Facilitator/Analyst ....

WEEKLY ITINERARY Language Facilitation Opportunities

Topic(s) of Focus: ______________________________

For the Week of: ____________________

	MORNING	MID- DAY	EVENING	MEALTIME
MONDAY				
TUESDAY				
WEDNESDAY				
THURSDAY				
FRIDAY				
SATURDAY				
SUNDAY				

UPCOMING EVENTS TO PLAN FOR:

BEST OPPORTUNITIES OF THE WEEK:

DAILY RECORD

Dates:

Topic(s) of Focus:

C=Connection / L=Listening / S = Speaking / M = Language Facilitator Mindset

MON

Daily Levels **Observations**

C L S M

TUE

Daily Levels **Observations**

C L S M

WED

Daily Levels **Observations**

C L S M

THU

Daily Levels **Observations**

C L S M

FRI

Daily Levels **Observations**

C L S M

SAT

Daily Levels **Observations**

C L S M

SUN

Daily Levels **Observations**

C L S M

What Changed This Week?

REFLECTIONS

Based on review of language facilitation experiences
for the week of:

This page is for you to write down whatever pops into your mind.

1. **Gratitude** *(What caused you to feel JOY this week?)*

2. **Blockages** *(What do you need to let go of?)*

3. **Intention** *(Where do you see potential to tap into with new action?)*

4. **Mindset** *(How do you feel about your current situation and your plan?)*

4. **Self Advice** *(What NEW action do YOU think will help improve your results?)*

SPOKEN LANGUAGE DEVELOPMENT **ANALYSIS/PLAN**

Based on review of language facilitation experiences for the week of:

▶ 1. ☐ Level of connection, attention, and listening to language models

▶ 2. ☐ Level of understanding and processing during language facilitation activities

▶ 3. ☐ Level of using speech for primary expression

This week's 3 most successful language facilitation opportunities:

▶ 4.

Plan for Progress

▶ 5.

Language Facilitator Mindset Level ☐

Strategy to Maintain a Positive Language Facilitation Environment

Strategy to Connect in the LF Zone and Facilitate Attention and Listening

Strategy to Facilitate Understanding and Processing of Speech

Strategy to Motivate Increased Effort to Talk

▶ Child's Name:

▶ Facilitator/Analyst

WEEKLY ITINERARY Language Facilitation Opportunities

Topic(s) of Focus: ______________________________

For the Week of: ____________________

	MORNING	MID- DAY	EVENING	MEALTIME
MONDAY				
TUESDAY				
WEDNESDAY				
THURSDAY				
FRIDAY				
SATURDAY				
SUNDAY				

UPCOMING EVENTS TO PLAN FOR:

BEST OPPORTUNITIES OF THE WEEK:

DAILY RECORD

Dates:

Topic(s) of Focus:

C=Connection / L=Listening / S = Speaking / M = Language Facilitator Mindset

MON

Daily Levels — C L S M

Observations

TUE

Daily Levels — C L S M

Observations

WED

Daily Levels — C L S M

Observations

THU

Daily Levels — C L S M

Observations

FRI

Daily Levels — C L S M

Observations

SAT

Daily Levels — C L S M

Observations

SUN

Daily Levels — C L S M

Observations

What Changed This Week?

REFLECTIONS

Based on review of language facilitation experiences for the week of:

This page is for you to write down whatever pops into your mind.

1. **Gratitude** *(What caused you to feel JOY this week?)*

2. **Blockages** *(What do you need to let go of?)*

3. **Intention** *(Where do you see potential to tap into with new action?)*

4. **Mindset** *(How do you feel about your current situation and your plan?)*

4. **Self Advice** *(What NEW action do YOU think will help improve your results?)*

Late Talker Profile

Get to know the late talker so you can see the world through their eyes.

NAME / AGE -

FREQUENT REQUESTS:
Activity, food, characters, color, music, clothes etc.

CURRENT FAVORITE -

FRUSTRATIONS -
What triggers feelings of Boredom, restriction, overwhelm, anxiety, embarrassment, fear

CURRENT ISSUES -

CURIOSITIES
What Toys, actions, topics do they explore on their own?

CURRENT FAVORITE -

COMFORTS:
Movement, sensory... What do they use for regulation and soothing?

CURRENT FAVORITE -

ANALYSIS OF STARTING LEVELS

- [ ] *Connection*
- [ ] *Listening*
- [ ] *Speaking*

OVERALL ATTITUDE ABOUT SPEECH

Language Facilitator Profile

Find your happiest path.

NAME / RELATIONSHIP TO THE LATE TALKER -

FREQUENT REQUESTS:
What do you need the late talker to do more independently to make life easier.

CURRENT WISH -

FRUSTRATIONS -
What triggers feelings of worry, restriction, overwhelm, anxiety, embarrassment, fear

CURRENT ISSUES -

CURIOSITIES
What do you find easy to do and enjoy learning more about?

CURRENT FAVORITE -

COMFORTS:
Movement, sensory...
What do YOU use for regulation and soothing?

CURRENT FAVORITE -

ANALYSIS OF STARTING MINDSET

☐ Mindset Level

Describe how you feel about your journey:

BIGGEST GOALS FOR YOUR JOURNEY

What do you intend to accomplish?

SPOKEN LANGUAGE DEVELOPMENT **ANALYSIS/PLAN**

Based on review of language facilitation experiences for the week of:

▸ 1. ☐ Level of connection, attention, and listening to language models

▸ 2. ☐ Level of understanding and processing during language facilitation activities

▸ 3. ☐ Level of using speech for primary expression

This week's 3 most successful language facilitation opportunities:

▸ 4.

Plan for Progress

▸ 5.

Language Facilitator Mindset Level ☐

Strategy to Maintain a Positive Language Facilitation Environment

Strategy to Connect in the LF Zone and Facilitate Attention and Listening

Strategy to Facilitate Understanding and Processing of Speech

Strategy to Motivate Increased Effort to Talk

▸ Child's Name:

▸ Facilitator/Analyst

WEEKLY ITINERARY Language Facilitation Opportunities

Topic(s) of Focus: ____________________

For the Week of: ____________________

	MORNING	MID- DAY	EVENING	MEALTIME
MONDAY				
TUESDAY				
WEDNESDAY				
THURSDAY				
FRIDAY				
SATURDAY				
SUNDAY				

UPCOMING EVENTS TO PLAN FOR:

BEST OPPORTUNITIES OF THE WEEK:

DAILY RECORD

Dates:

Topic(s) of Focus:

C=Connection / L=Listening / S = Speaking / M = Language Facilitator Mindset

MON

Daily Levels **Observations**

C L S M

TUE

Daily Levels **Observations**

C L S M

WED

Daily Levels **Observations**

C L S M

THU

Daily Levels **Observations**

C L S M

FRI

Daily Levels **Observations**

C L S M

SAT

Daily Levels **Observations**

C L S M

SUN

Daily Levels **Observations**

C L S M

What Changed This Week?

REFLECTIONS

Based on review of language facilitation experiences for the week of:

This page is for you to write down whatever pops into your mind.

1. **Gratitude** *(What caused you to feel JOY this week?)*

2. **Blockages** *(What do you need to let go of?)*

3. **Intention** *(Where do you see potential to tap into with new action?)*

4. **Mindset** *(How do you feel about your current situation and your plan?)*

4. **Self Advice** *(What NEW action do YOU think will help improve your results?)*

SPOKEN LANGUAGE DEVELOPMENT **ANALYSIS/PLAN**

Based on review of language facilitation experiences for the week of:

▶ 1. ☐ Level of connection, attention, and listening to language models

▶ 2. ☐ Level of understanding and processing during language facilitation activities

▶ 3. ☐ Level of using speech for primary expression

This week's 3 most successful language facilitation opportunities:

▶ 4.

Plan for Progress

▶ 5.

Language Facilitator Mindset Level ☐

Strategy to Maintain a Positive Language Facilitation Environment

Strategy to Connect in the LF Zone and Facilitate Attention and Listening

Strategy to Facilitate Understanding and Processing of Speech

Strategy to Motivate Increased Effort to Talk

▶ Child's Name:

▶ Facilitator/Analyst

WEEKLY ITINERARY Language Facilitation Opportunities

Topic(s) of Focus: ______________________________

For the Week of: ____________________

	MORNING	MID- DAY	EVENING	MEALTIME
MONDAY				
TUESDAY				
WEDNESDAY				
THURSDAY				
FRIDAY				
SATURDAY				
SUNDAY				

UPCOMING EVENTS TO PLAN FOR:

BEST OPPORTUNITIES OF THE WEEK:

DAILY RECORD

Dates: ______

Topic(s) of Focus: ______

C=Connection / L=Listening / S = Speaking / M = Language Facilitator Mindset

MON

Daily Levels — Observations

C	L	S	M

TUE

Daily Levels — Observations

C	L	S	M

WED

Daily Levels — Observations

C	L	S	M

THU

Daily Levels — Observations

C	L	S	M

FRI

Daily Levels — Observations

C	L	S	M

SAT

Daily Levels — Observations

C	L	S	M

SUN

Daily Levels — Observations

C	L	S	M

What Changed This Week?

REFLECTIONS

Based on review of language facilitation experiences for the week of:

This page is for you to write down whatever pops into your mind.

1. **Gratitude** *(What caused you to feel JOY this week?)*

2. **Blockages** *(What do you need to let go of?)*

3. **Intention** *(Where do you see potential to tap into with new action?)*

4. **Mindset** *(How do you feel about your current situation and your plan?)*

4. **Self Advice** *(What NEW action do YOU think will help improve your results?)*

SPOKEN LANGUAGE DEVELOPMENT **ANALYSIS/PLAN**

Based on review of language facilitation experiences for the week of:

____

▶ 1. ☐ Level of connection, attention, and listening to language models

▶ 2. ☐ Level of understanding and processing during language facilitation activities

▶ 3. ☐ Level of using speech for primary expression

This week's 3 most successful language facilitation opportunities:

▶ 4.

Plan for Progress

▶ 5.

Language Facilitator Mindset Level ☐

Strategy to Maintain a Positive Language Facilitation Environment

Strategy to Connect in the LF Zone and Facilitate Attention and Listening

Strategy to Facilitate Understanding and Processing of Speech

Strategy to Motivate Increased Effort to Talk

▶ Child's Name:

▶ Facilitator/Analyst

WEEKLY ITINERARY Language Facilitation Opportunities

Topic(s) of Focus: ______________________________

For the Week of: ____________________

	MORNING	MID- DAY	EVENING	MEALTIME
MONDAY				
TUESDAY				
WEDNESDAY				
THURSDAY				
FRIDAY				
SATURDAY				
SUNDAY				

UPCOMING EVENTS TO PLAN FOR:

BEST OPPORTUNITIES OF THE WEEK:

DAILY RECORD

Dates:

Topic(s) of Focus:

C=Connection / L=Listening / S = Speaking / M = Language Facilitator Mindset

MON

Daily Levels — Observations

C	L	S	M

TUE

Daily Levels — Observations

C	L	S	M

WED

Daily Levels — Observations

C	L	S	M

THU

Daily Levels — Observations

C	L	S	M

FRI

Daily Levels — Observations

C	L	S	M

SAT

Daily Levels — Observations

C	L	S	M

SUN

Daily Levels — Observations

C	L	S	M

What Changed This Week?

REFLECTIONS

Based on review of language facilitation experiences for the week of:

This page is for you to write down whatever pops into your mind.

1. **Gratitude** *(What caused you to feel JOY this week?)*

2. **Blockages** *(What do you need to let go of?)*

3. **Intention** *(Where do you see potential to tap into with new action?)*

4. **Mindset** *(How do you feel about your current situation and your plan?)*

4. **Self Advice** *(What NEW action do YOU think will help improve your results?)*

Late Talker Profile

Get to know the late talker so you can see the world through their eyes.

NAME / AGE -

FREQUENT REQUESTS:
Activity, food, characters, color, music, clothes etc.

CURRENT FAVORITE -

FRUSTRATIONS -
What triggers feelings of Boredom, restriction, overwhelm, anxiety, embarrassment, fear

CURRENT ISSUES -

CURIOSITIES
What Toys, actions, topics do they explore on their own?

CURRENT FAVORITE -

COMFORTS:
Movement, sensory... What do they use for regulation and soothing?

CURRENT FAVORITE -

ANALYSIS OF STARTING LEVELS

- [ ] *Connection*
- [ ] *Listening*
- [ ] *Speaking*

OVERALL ATTITUDE ABOUT SPEECH

Language Facilitator Profile

Find your happiest path.

NAME / RELATIONSHIP TO THE LATE TALKER -

FREQUENT REQUESTS:
What do you need the late talker to do more independently to make life easier.

CURRENT WISH -

FRUSTRATIONS -
What triggers feelings of worry, restriction, overwhelm, anxiety, embarrassment, fear

CURRENT ISSUES -

CURIOSITIES
What do you find easy to do and enjoy learning more about?

CURRENT FAVORITE -

COMFORTS:
Movement, sensory...
What do YOU use for regulation and soothing?

CURRENT FAVORITE -

ANALYSIS OF STARTING MINDSET

☐ Mindset Level

Describe how you feel about your journey:

BIGGEST GOALS FOR YOUR JOURNEY

What do you intend to accomplish?

SPOKEN LANGUAGE DEVELOPMENT **ANALYSIS/PLAN**

Based on review of language facilitation experiences for the week of:

▶ 1. ☐ Level of connection, attention, and listening to language models

▶ 2. ☐ Level of understanding and processing during language facilitation activities

▶ 3. ☐ Level of using speech for primary expression

This week's 3 most successful language facilitation opportunities:

▶ 4.

Plan for Progress

▶ 5.

Language Facilitator Mindset Level ☐

Strategy to Maintain a Positive Language Facilitation Environment

Strategy to Connect in the LF Zone and Facilitate Attention and Listening

Strategy to Facilitate Understanding and Processing of Speech

Strategy to Motivate Increased Effort to Talk

▶ Child's Name:

▶ Facilitator/Analyst

WEEKLY ITINERARY Language Facilitation Opportunities

Topic(s) of Focus: ______________________________

For the Week of: ____________________

	MORNING	MID- DAY	EVENING	MEALTIME
MONDAY				
TUESDAY				
WEDNESDAY				
THURSDAY				
FRIDAY				
SATURDAY				
SUNDAY				

UPCOMING EVENTS TO PLAN FOR:

BEST OPPORTUNITIES OF THE WEEK:

DAILY RECORD

Dates:

Topic(s) of Focus:

C=Connection / L=Listening / S = Speaking / M = Language Facilitator Mindset

MON

Daily Levels C L S M

Observations

TUE

Daily Levels C L S M

Observations

WED

Daily Levels C L S M

Observations

THU

Daily Levels C L S M

Observations

FRI

Daily Levels C L S M

Observations

SAT

Daily Levels C L S M

Observations

SUN

Daily Levels C L S M

Observations

What Changed This Week?

REFLECTIONS

Based on review of language facilitation experiences for the week of:

This page is for you to write down whatever pops into your mind.

1. **Gratitude** *(What caused you to feel JOY this week?)*

2. **Blockages** *(What do you need to let go of?)*

3. **Intention** *(Where do you see potential to tap into with new action?)*

4. **Mindset** *(How do you feel about your current situation and your plan?)*

4. **Self Advice** *(What NEW action do YOU think will help improve your results?)*

SPOKEN LANGUAGE DEVELOPMENT **ANALYSIS/PLAN**

Based on review of language facilitation experiences for the week of:

▶ 1. ☐ Level of connection, attention, and listening to language models

▶ 2. ☐ Level of understanding and processing during language facilitation activities

▶ 3. ☐ Level of using speech for primary expression

This week's 3 most successful language facilitation opportunities:

▶ 4.

Plan for Progress

▶ 5.

Language Facilitator Mindset Level ☐

Strategy to Maintain a Positive Language Facilitation Environment

Strategy to Connect in the LF Zone and Facilitate Attention and Listening

Strategy to Facilitate Understanding and Processing of Speech

Strategy to Motivate Increased Effort to Talk

▶ Child's Name:

▶ Facilitator/Analyst

WEEKLY ITINERARY Language Facilitation Opportunities

Topic(s) of Focus: ______________________________

For the Week of: ____________________

	MORNING	MID- DAY	EVENING	MEALTIME
MONDAY				
TUESDAY				
WEDNESDAY				
THURSDAY				
FRIDAY				
SATURDAY				
SUNDAY				

UPCOMING EVENTS TO PLAN FOR:

BEST OPPORTUNITIES OF THE WEEK:

DAILY RECORD

Dates:

Topic(s) of Focus:

C=Connection / L=Listening / S = Speaking / M = Language Facilitator Mindset

MON

Daily Levels — C L S M

Observations

TUE

Daily Levels — C L S M

Observations

WED

Daily Levels — C L S M

Observations

THU

Daily Levels — C L S M

Observations

FRI

Daily Levels — C L S M

Observations

SAT

Daily Levels — C L S M

Observations

SUN

Daily Levels — C L S M

Observations

What Changed This Week?

REFLECTIONS

Based on review of language facilitation experiences for the week of:

____

This page is for you to write down whatever pops into your mind.

1. **Gratitude** *(What caused you to feel JOY this week?)*

2. **Blockages** *(What do you need to let go of?)*

3. **Intention** *(Where do you see potential to tap into with new action?)*

4. **Mindset** *(How do you feel about your current situation and your plan?)*

4. **Self Advice** *(What NEW action do YOU think will help improve your results?)*

SPOKEN LANGUAGE DEVELOPMENT **ANALYSIS/PLAN**

Based on review of language facilitation experiences for the week of:

____

▶ 1.	☐ Level of connection, attention, and listening to language models
▶ 2.	☐ Level of understanding and processing during language facilitation activities
▶ 3.	☐ Level of using speech for primary expression

This week's 3 most successful language facilitation opportunities:

▶ 4.

Plan for Progress ▶ 5. Language Facilitator Mindset Level ☐	Strategy to Maintain a Positive Language Facilitation Environment Strategy to Connect in the LF Zone and Facilitate Attention and Listening Strategy to Facilitate Understanding and Processing of Speech Strategy to Motivate Increased Effort to Talk

▶ Child's Name: ....

▶ Facilitator/Analyst ....

WEEKLY ITINERARY Language Facilitation Opportunities

Topic(s) of Focus: ______________________________

For the Week of: ____________________

	MORNING	MID- DAY	EVENING	MEALTIME
MONDAY				
TUESDAY				
WEDNESDAY				
THURSDAY				
FRIDAY				
SATURDAY				
SUNDAY				

UPCOMING EVENTS TO PLAN FOR:

BEST OPPORTUNITIES OF THE WEEK:

DAILY RECORD

Dates:

Topic(s) of Focus:

C=Connection / L=Listening / S = Speaking / M = Language Facilitator Mindset

MON

Daily Levels **Observations**

C	L	S	M

TUE

Daily Levels **Observations**

C	L	S	M

WED

Daily Levels **Observations**

C	L	S	M

THU

Daily Levels **Observations**

C	L	S	M

FRI

Daily Levels **Observations**

C	L	S	M

SAT

Daily Levels **Observations**

C	L	S	M

SUN

Daily Levels **Observations**

C	L	S	M

What Changed This Week?

REFLECTIONS

Based on review of language facilitation experiences
for the week of:

____

This page is for you to write down whatever pops into your mind.

1. **Gratitude** *(What caused you to feel JOY this week?)*

2. **Blockages** *(What do you need to let go of?)*

3. **Intention** *(Where do you see potential to tap into with new action?)*

4. **Mindset** *(How do you feel about your current situation and your plan?)*

4. **Self Advice** *(What NEW action do YOU think will help improve your results?)*

Late Talker Profile

Get to know the late talker so you can see the world through their eyes.

NAME / AGE -

FREQUENT REQUESTS:
Activity, food, characters, color, music, clothes etc.

CURRENT FAVORITE -

FRUSTRATIONS -
What triggers feelings of Boredom, restriction, overwhelm, anxiety, embarrassment, fear

CURRENT ISSUES -

CURIOSITIES
What Toys, actions, topics do they explore on their own?

CURRENT FAVORITE -

COMFORTS:
Movement, sensory... What do they use for regulation and soothing?

CURRENT FAVORITE -

ANALYSIS OF STARTING LEVELS

- ☐ *Connection*
- ☐ *Listening*
- ☐ *Speaking*

OVERALL ATTITUDE ABOUT SPEECH

Language Facilitator Profile

Find your happiest path.

NAME / RELATIONSHIP TO THE LATE TALKER -

FREQUENT REQUESTS:
What do you need the late talker to do more independently to make life easier.

CURRENT WISH -

FRUSTRATIONS -
What triggers feelings of worry, restriction, overwhelm, anxiety, embarrassment, fear

CURRENT ISSUES -

CURIOSITIES
What do you find easy to do and enjoy learning more about?

CURRENT FAVORITE -

COMFORTS:
Movement, sensory...
What do YOU use for regulation and soothing?

CURRENT FAVORITE -

ANALYSIS OF STARTING MINDSET

☐ Mindset Level

Describe how you feel about your journey:

BIGGEST GOALS FOR YOUR JOURNEY

What do you intend to accomplish?

SPOKEN LANGUAGE DEVELOPMENT **ANALYSIS/PLAN**

Based on review of language facilitation experiences for the week of:

▸ 1. ☐ Level of connection, attention, and listening to language models

▸ 2. ☐ Level of understanding and processing during language facilitation activities

▸ 3. ☐ Level of using speech for primary expression

This week's 3 most successful language facilitation opportunities:

▸ 4.

Plan for Progress

▸ 5.

Language Facilitator Mindset Level ☐

Strategy to Maintain a Positive Language Facilitation Environment

Strategy to Connect in the LF Zone and Facilitate Attention and Listening

Strategy to Facilitate Understanding and Processing of Speech

Strategy to Motivate Increased Effort to Talk

▸ Child's Name:

▸ Facilitator/Analyst

WEEKLY ITINERARY Language Facilitation Opportunities

Topic(s) of Focus: ________________

For the Week of: ________________

	MORNING	MID- DAY	EVENING	MEALTIME
MONDAY				
TUESDAY				
WEDNESDAY				
THURSDAY				
FRIDAY				
SATURDAY				
SUNDAY				

UPCOMING EVENTS TO PLAN FOR:

BEST OPPORTUNITIES OF THE WEEK:

DAILY RECORD

Dates:

Topic(s) of Focus:

C=Connection / L=Listening / S = Speaking / M = Language Facilitator Mindset

MON	Daily Levels				Observations
	C	L	S	M	

TUE	Daily Levels				Observations
	C	L	S	M	

WED	Daily Levels				Observations
	C	L	S	M	

THU	Daily Levels				Observations
	C	L	S	M	

FRI	Daily Levels				Observations
	C	L	S	M	

SAT	Daily Levels				Observations
	C	L	S	M	

SUN	Daily Levels				Observations
	C	L	S	M	

What Changed This Week?

REFLECTIONS

Based on review of language facilitation experiences for the week of:

This page is for you to write down whatever pops into your mind.

1. **Gratitude** *(What caused you to feel JOY this week?)*

2. **Blockages** *(What do you need to let go of?)*

3. **Intention** *(Where do you see potential to tap into with new action?)*

4. **Mindset** *(How do you feel about your current situation and your plan?)*

4. **Self Advice** *(What NEW action do YOU think will help improve your results?)*

SPOKEN LANGUAGE DEVELOPMENT **ANALYSIS/PLAN**

Based on review of language facilitation experiences for the week of:

▶ 1.	☐ Level of connection, attention, and listening to language models
▶ 2.	☐ Level of understanding and processing during language facilitation activities
▶ 3.	☐ Level of using speech for primary expression

This week's 3 most successful language facilitation opportunities: ▶ 4.

Plan for Progress

▶ 5.

Language Facilitator Mindset Level ☐

Strategy to Maintain a Positive Language Facilitation Environment

Strategy to Connect in the LF Zone and Facilitate Attention and Listening

Strategy to Facilitate Understanding and Processing of Speech

Strategy to Motivate Increased Effort to Talk

▶ Child's Name:

▶ Facilitator/Analyst

WEEKLY ITINERARY Language Facilitation Opportunities

Topic(s) of Focus: ______________________

For the Week of: ______________________

	MORNING	MID- DAY	EVENING	MEALTIME
MONDAY				
TUESDAY				
WEDNESDAY				
THURSDAY				
FRIDAY				
SATURDAY				
SUNDAY				

UPCOMING EVENTS TO PLAN FOR:

BEST OPPORTUNITIES OF THE WEEK:

DAILY RECORD

Dates: ____________

Topic(s) of Focus: ____________

C=Connection / L=Listening / S = Speaking / M = Language Facilitator Mindset

MON

Daily Levels C L S M

Observations

TUE

Daily Levels C L S M

Observations

WED

Daily Levels C L S M

Observations

THU

Daily Levels C L S M

Observations

FRI

Daily Levels C L S M

Observations

SAT

Daily Levels C L S M

Observations

SUN

Daily Levels C L S M

Observations

What Changed This Week?

REFLECTIONS

Based on review of language facilitation experiences for the week of:

This page is for you to write down whatever pops into your mind.

1. **Gratitude** *(What caused you to feel JOY this week?)*

2. **Blockages** *(What do you need to let go of?)*

3. **Intention** *(Where do you see potential to tap into with new action?)*

4. **Mindset** *(How do you feel about your current situation and your plan?)*

4. **Self Advice** *(What NEW action do YOU think will help improve your results?)*

Late Talker Profile

Get to know the late talker so you can see the world through their eyes.

NAME / AGE -

FREQUENT REQUESTS:
Activity, food, characters, color, music, clothes etc.

CURRENT FAVORITE -

FRUSTRATIONS -
What triggers feelings of Boredom, restriction, overwhelm, anxiety, embarrassment, fear

CURRENT ISSUES -

CURIOSITIES
What Toys, actions, topics do they explore on their own?

CURRENT FAVORITE -

COMFORTS:
Movement, sensory... What do they use for regulation and soothing?

CURRENT FAVORITE -

ANALYSIS OF STARTING LEVELS

- [ ] *Connection*
- [ ] *Listening*
- [ ] *Speaking*

OVERALL ATTITUDE ABOUT SPEECH

Language Facilitator Profile

Find your happiest path.

NAME / RELATIONSHIP TO THE LATE TALKER -

FREQUENT REQUESTS:
What do you need the late talker to do more independently to make life easier.

CURRENT WISH -

FRUSTRATIONS -
What triggers feelings of worry, restriction, overwhelm, anxiety, embarrassment, fear

CURRENT ISSUES -

CURIOSITIES
What do you find easy to do and enjoy learning more about?

CURRENT FAVORITE -

COMFORTS:
Movement, sensory...
What do YOU use for regulation and soothing?

CURRENT FAVORITE -

ANALYSIS OF STARTING MINDSET

☐ Mindset Level

Describe how you feel about your journey:

BIGGEST GOALS FOR YOUR JOURNEY

What do you intend to accomplish?

How Did You Facilitate Progress?

First Month Highlights	What Changed?

Second Month Highlights	What Changed?

Third Month Highlights	What Changed?

Mindset Changes

What New Habits Have Developed?
(What habits have you let go of?)

Lessons Learned From the Late Talker

What Happens After 11 Weeks?

Celebrate How Far You Have Come

Your documentation provides the data you need to see exactly how your efforts have helped you progress on your lifetime journey. Review everything you have written in your journal for the past 11 weeks and notice how different you feel. Recognize that YOU are the cause of your reality now and every day.

Realize You Have Only Just Begun

Your newly developed language facilitation habits have shown you how powerful you are. Now you may feel more prepared to take on any new challenge that comes your way and explore new ideas with an open, conscious language facilitator mindset. Functional spoken language expertise takes YEARS to develop and in fact we never stop learning as long as there are new opportunities presented. This late talker has come to rely on you as the source of their language learning and they need you to continue on your journey together.

Decide How You Will Move Forward

Did the Structure Work for You?

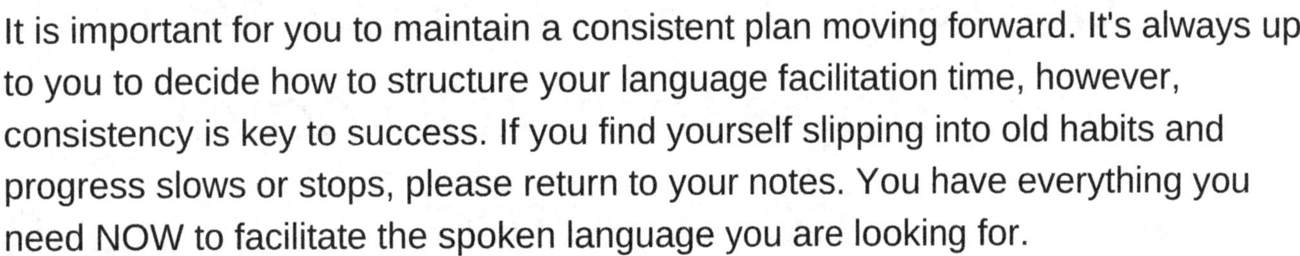

It is important for you to maintain a consistent plan moving forward. It's always up to you to decide how to structure your language facilitation time, however, consistency is key to success. If you find yourself slipping into old habits and progress slows or stops, please return to your notes. You have everything you need NOW to facilitate the spoken language you are looking for.

Please consider contacting me to share your experience. You are always welcome to comment on a video, reach out on social media, or send my team an email. Support@WavesofCommunication.com

Congratulations!

PRACTICE GRATITUDE

It is time to celebrate and show gratitude for the connection and success in the spoken language that YOU have co-created.

Please SHARE Your Success!

Share your experience with other parents and caregivers to help them understand the power of language facilitation.

Kindly Leave a review of this workbook on Amazon

Your work is helping a late talking child learn to share their wisdom with the world.

That makes the world a better place for all of us.

Thank You!

~Marci Melzer

Made in the USA
Las Vegas, NV
04 January 2025

15898529R00070